Grand Duchess Maria Nikolayevna and her Palace in St. Petersburg

in painting and graphic work from
the best museum collections of

The HERMITAGE,
The STATE RUSSIAN MUSEUM,
RUSSIA'S ART ACADEMY,
the Palace-Museums
of TSARSKOYE SELO,
GATCHINA, etc.

Unique material
from the family lore
of the Dukes of Leuchtenberg

Contents

Introduction
5

Grand Duchess Maria and Maximilian
Duke of Leuchtenberg
17

Construction of the Maryinsky Palace
45

Maria's family home
69

Descendants of Maria and Maximilian,
Princes Romanovsky Dukes of Leuchtenberg
203

Maryinsky Palace during the time
of the Imperial Council, and after 1917
231

Notes. Select Bibliography
240

Grand Duchess Maria Nikolayevna and her Palace in St. Petersburg

Zoia Belyakova

Photography LEONID BOGDANOV

Design and layout
LIUBOV RAKHMILEVICH

EGO Publishers • St.Petersburg

Consultants:

Prof. TATIANA SLAVINA,
Academican, Ph.D. (architecture)

SERGEI SEMENTSOV,
M.Sc. (architecture)

English text edited by SANDRA STOTT

Editor-general IRENE FRESHKO

EVGENI ANTONENKO
Photos Nos 6, 7, 9—12, 42—44,
164, 167, 178, 182, 184, 186, 193

Type-setting & design
ALEXANDER PETROV

PRINTED AND BOUND IN FINLAND, Tornio

COLOUR SEPARATION BY OULUREPRO Ltd, FINLAND

ISBN 5-82-76-0011-3

ACKNOWLEDGEMENTS

I am much indebted to all the people who helped me in the preparation of this book. In St. Petersburg, I am particularly grateful to the staff of EGO Publishing who enthusiastically materialized the book project under the current deplorable economic conditions. I also thank the researchers of the Art Academy, the Pushkin House, the Russian Museum (drawing department), and Adel Jolkina (Curator of Gatchina Palace) who helped to collect material for photography in this book. I especially thank Liubov Isachenko and Boris Asvarishch from the Hermitage for their valuable suggestions and useful leads at moments of discouragement.

In England and the USA, I wish to express my gratitude to many friends who offered hospitality both generous and timely, and made my research work at the libraries in London and Washington possible. I am particularly grateful to Peter Lauritzen (Venice), an erudite and resplendent art historian, who, a few years ago, happened to read my short article on the Grand Duchess and her palace. From the outset, he encouraged me to make the article into an accomplished book.

Russian traditional low bow to the living descendants of Maria and Maximilian the Duke of Leuchtenberg: Nicholas von Leuchtenberg (Germany), Maria de Pasquale (USA), Xenia Grabbe and her husband Dmitri (USA) who provided me with family records and invaluable illustrations and put their incomparable memory at my disposal.

Finally, I am much grateful to my husband Leonid Belyakov for his patience and support, and especially for his understanding of the striving demands of the academic author, wife and mistress of the house.

*HE WHO IS CURIOUS
ABOUT HIS ANCESTORS
IS WORTHY OF HIS MOTHERLAND*

N.M.Karamzin

What would have surprised a traveller visiting St. Petersburg a century or so ago? Not only a great number of rivers, canals and islands. After all, there are more of them in Venice or Amsterdam. A European visitor would have been quite delighted with its architecture, the gorgeous ensembles, with the splendour of the numerous palaces owned by members of the Imperial family. Even today, the former Romanov residences still imbue St. Petersburg with a particular beauty of its own.

The Marble Palace happened to be the first palatial gift in the northern capital offered to a grand duke. It was built by Catherine II for her favourite Count Grigory Orlov. It was later purchased from his heirs and, in February, 1796, presented to her grandson Grand Duke Constantine on the occasion of his wedding. The Romanovs continued to build residences for their children during the first half of the 19th century, so that by the end of the last century there were more than twenty lavish palaces in their possession. These were ideally located in the most picturesque squares and on the river embankments, the spots so celebrated by both poets and artists.[1]

In comparison, Queen Victoria of Great Britain and Ireland, who ruled from 1837 to 1901, occupied together with her huge family only five residences in London of which Buckingham and St. James' palaces are the best known. The Queen referred to her other residences as 'houses'. It is seldom realized that Buckingham Palace only acquired its current palatial dimensions in the 20th century. The Emperors and Kings of France — Napoléon I, Louis XVIII, Charles X, Napoléon III — all contented themselves with life in the Tuileries Palace in Paris. The Bourbon Palace had been used as a governmental office since the time of Napoléon I, and the Louvre had been transformed into the National Museum after the events of 1791—93. In the Paris Commune days of 1871, the Tuileries was destroyed. France became a Republic with a President. All together such dynasties as the Hapsburgs of Austria-Hungary, the Hohenzollerns of Germany, the Bourbons of Spain and the Savoys of Italy could not boast such an abundance of private palaces in their own capitals. Only the Romanovs, who were the last absolute monarchs of unlimited power in Europe, went on building the palaces of the grand dukes with unfailing lavish extravagance.

At first, the most eminent architects built these residences for the Emperor's sons: the Grand Duke Michael's Palace for the youngest son of Emperor Paul, the Grand Duke Nicholas' and New-Michael's Palaces for the younger sons of Emperor Nicholas I, along with a palace on the embankment of the Neva river for Grand Duke Vladimir, son of Emperor Alexander II. Later, when the city had expanded considerably and dense overbuilding had to be taken into account, they began to buy private mansions from individual owners and refurbished them in the latest fashion. These magnificently renewed residences were presented to the sons and grandsons of the Emperor. Thus, in 1884, a palace was bought from the Belosselsky-Belozersky princes for Grand Duke Serge; in 1881 and 1889, private houses belonging to the Saburov and Stiglits families were bought for Grand Dukes Alexis and Paul, all three younger sons of Alexander II. In 1894, a house was purchased from Princess Maria Vorontsova for the grandson of Nicholas I, Grand Duke Alexander and his wife Grand Duchess Xenia, the sister of the last Emperor.

No palaces were ever built for the Tsar's daughters, the grand duchesses of Russia. They married foreign princes of prominent sovereign families and their destiny, as a rule, was to live away from Russia. The House of Romanov counted twenty three grand duchesses by birth who reached adulthood in the 19th-20th centuries. Almost all of them left Russia upon their marriage into other dynasties, except for eight girls: Nicholas I's daughter Maria and his niece Maria who was not betrothed and died early, the last

Emperor's sisters Olga and Xenia, who lived in Russia after their marriage, and his four daughters who were killed by the Bolsheviks.

The favourite eldest daughter of Emperor Nicholas I was an exception. The Maryinsky Palace in St. Isaac's Square which was specially erected for Grand Duchess Maria Nikolayevna may be described as the only residence built for a Tsar's daughter. Its construction which began in summer 1839 makes for one of the most captivating stories of palatial architecture in St. Petersburg.

The history of this building is inextricably linked with the individuality and destiny of its owners and in fact lacks sense when taken separately. The lifestyle, character and taste of the owner commands the identity and spirit of any home. The Maryinsky state rooms rivalled the Tsar's own in their uniqueness, and were extraordinary as the three patrons of the project were most extraordinary, the Sovereign, his daughter and his son-in-law, the then President of the Art Academy, in their unlimited finance, erudition and taste. The harmonious unity of their intentions, preferences and the possibilities available to them and of the talent and experience of the chosen architect may explain why the first independent commission in the capital for the architect Stakenschneider happened to become his best accomplishment.

1 **The Marble Palace** (1768—85, arch. A.Rinaldi) on the Palace Embankment of the Neva river, No 4. Residence of the Grand Dukes, Constantine Pavlovich, Constantine Nikolayevich and Constantine Constantinovich.

2 **Michael's Palace** (Mikhailovsky, 1819—25, arch. Carlo Rossi) in Mikhailovsky Square. Residence of Grand Duke Michael Pavlovich, son of Emperor Paul I. The State Russian Museum at present.

3 **Grand Duke Nicholas' Palace** (Nikolayevsky, 1853—61, arch. A.Stakenschneider) in Annunciation Square. Residence of Grand Duke Nicholas Nikolayevich, Sr., son of Emperor Nicholas I.

4 **New Michael's Palace** (Novo-Mikhailovsky, 1858—61, arch. A.Stakenschneider) on the Palace Embankment, No 18. Residence of Grand Duke Michael Nikolayevich, son of Emperor Nicholas I.

5 **Grand Duke Vladimir's Palace** (1867—72, arch. A.Rezanov) on the Palace Embankment, No 26. Residence of Grand Duke Vladimir Alexandrovich, son of Emperor Alexander II.

6 **Grand Duke Alexis' Palace** (former mansion of A.I.Saburov, 1846—48, arch. N.Yefimov, rebuilt by M.Mesmakher) on the Moika river, No 122. Residence of Grand Duke Alexis Alexandrovich, son of Emperor Alexander II.

7 **A monumental wrought-iron railing** embellished with spears, tridents and the Grand Duke's monogram A&A. The exquisite lattice was commissioned to San Galle works at a price of 44,959 roubles. Grand Duke Alexis, the then Grand Admiral and Head of the Naval Department, preferred to reside not in a central part of the capital, but in a traditional maritime outskirt, and in a mansion refurbished as a romantic medieval castle adorned with towers. His residence happened to be the last palatial estate in St. Petersburg.

8 **Grand Duke Serge's Palace** (palace of the Belosselsky-Belozersky family, 1846—48, arch. A. Stakenschneider) on Nevsky Avenue, No 41. Purchased for Grand Duke Serge Alexandrovich, son of Emperor Alexander II.

9 **Grand Duke Paul's Palace** (former mansion of Baron A.L.Stiglits, 1859—62, arch. G.Crakau. Rebuilt by M.Mesmakher in 1889) on the English Embankment, No 68. Purchased for Grand Duke Paul Alexandrovich, son of Emperor Alexander II.

10 An element of Classical decoration on the main façade. The palace design is in the style of the late Renaissance revival. It is a two-storey building, not only higher than the neighbouring three-storey house, but towering over the whole construction site on this part of the English Embankment.

11 **Palace of Grand Duchess Xenia** (former mansion of Countess M.Vorontsova, rebuilt in 1894—95) on the Moika Embankment, No 106. Purchased for Grand Duchess Xenia Alexandrovna, sister of the last Emperor Nicholas II, and her husband Grand Duke Alexander Mikhailovich, grandson of Emperor Nicholas I.

12 The Palace now houses the P.F.Lesgaft Academy of Physical Culture and is in poor condition.

Three palaces (6, 9, 11) are in deplorable condition. Nothing spared them from plunder and destruction after October 1917. They accomodated orphanages and homes for juvenile offenders, military offices, driving schools, etc. Hence, black & white illustrations have been preferred and additional pictures evincing their former splendour.

THE ROMANOV IMPERIAL HOUSE.

Children and grandchildren of Emperor Nicholas I and Empress Alexandra Feodorovna

Nicholas I (1796—1855) ∞ Alexandra Feodorovna Pr. of Prussia (1798—1860)

- **Alexander II** (1818—81)
  - ∞ Maria Alexandrovna Pr. of Hesse-Darmstadt (1824—80)
    - Alexandra (1842—49)
    - Nicholas (1843—65)
    - Alexander III (1845—94)
    - Vladimir (1847—1909)
    - Alexis (1850—1908)
    - Marie (1853—1920)
    - Serge (1857—1905)
    - Paul (1860—1919)
  - ∞ Ser. Highness Pr. C.M. Yurievsky (née Pr. C. Dolgoruky) (1847—1922)
    - Princes Yurievsky:
    - George (1872—1913)
    - Olga (1873—1925)
    - Catherine (1878—1959)
- **Maria** (1819—76)
  - ∞ Maximilian 3rd D. of Leuchtenberg (1817—52)
    - Alexandra (1840—43)
    - Maria (1841—1914)
    - Nicholas (1843—90)
    - Eugenia (1845—1925)
    - Evguen (1847—1901)
    - Sergei (1849—77)
    - George (1852—1912)
  - ∞ Grigory, Count Stroganov (1823—78)
    - Helen (1861—1908)
- **Olga** (1822—92)
  - ∞ Charles I of Württemberg Her. Pr., later King (1823—91)
    - Württemberg dynasty
- **Alexandra** (1825—44)
  - ∞ Lgr. of Hesse-Kassel (1820—84)
- **Constantine** (1827—92)
  - ∞ Alexandra Iosifovna Pr. of Saxe-Altenburg (1830—1911)
    - Nicholas (1850—1918)
    - Olga (1851—1926)
    - Vera (1854—1912)
    - Constantine (1858—1915)
    - Dmitri (1860—1919)
    - Viacheslav (1862—79)
- **Nicholas, Sr.** (1831—91)
  - ∞ Alexandra Petrovna Pr. of Oldenburg (1838—1900)
    - Nicholas, Jr. (1856—1929)
    - Peter (1864—1931)
- **Michael** (1832—1909)
  - ∞ Olga Feodorovna Pr. of Baden (1839—91)
    - Nicholas (1859—1919)
    - Anastasia (1860—1922)
    - Michael (1861—1929)
    - George (1863—1919)
    - Alexander (1866—1933)
    - Serge (1869—1918)
    - Alexis (1875—95)

Grand Duchess Maria and Maximilian Duke of Leuchtenberg

Grand Duchess Maria was born in Krasnoye Selo near Petersburg on 6(18) August 1819 and grew up together with her sisters Olga and Alexandra. Memoirs describe the 'informal childhood' of the little princesses. Governors noted the simplicity and severity of the surroundings: the girls' rooms on the ground floor of the Winter Palace were void of any tsarish luxury. A watercolour taken from the Romanov private album shows the room Maria had as a young girl to be unpretentious, yet, refined in its decor. Their parents, whilst affectionate towards the children, never overindulged or spoilt them. The Emperor always remembered that the likely prospect of marriage into a not too wealthy German royal family would make such a drastic contrast to their life at the Russian court: the most magnificent and sumptuous court in Europe.

Fresh air for the girls was prescribed in all seasons, and doctors controlled their diet. Classes began at 8:00 a.m. Until 1839, the liberal Privy Chancellor and poet Vasili Zhukovsky was responsible for the grand duchesses' tuition and education, and according to Alexander Turgenev, acted as a 'child's Aristotle' aiming as he did to cultivate in his royal wards respect for individuality and true Christian love towards one another. Zhukovsky remained their close friend and literary adviser right up until his death.

Dancing and drawing lessons were arranged together with Tsesarevich Alexander and his élite companions.[2] Their drawing tutor was the artist Zauderweid who used to accompany Nicholas I on his travels throughout Europe and Russia. Maria's sketch-book which amazingly has survived and is in the hands of her descendants (they live in the USA) shows her progress and drawing skills in 1826—30. Maria also painted fairly well and eventually had lessons with the artist A.G.Ukhtomsky. Later Maria became an enlightened benefactress of the arts and a collector of art works. All three girls delighted everyone with their cordiality, amiability, with their impeccable manners, gracefulness and musical capabilities.

The children of Nicholas I and Alexandra Feodorovna grew up very attached to one another. There was a genuine fondness between them and they remained devoted friends even after they had all married and lived apart. Most touching was the affection of Tsesarevich Alexander towards Maria and Olga. In his teens, while travelling in Europe in the company of his mentor Zhukovsky, Alexander missed his sisters terribly and wrote to them almost every day.

The children benefited from the extraordinary warmth and accord instilled in the immediate family by Empress Alexandra. It is well known that Catherine II reared her grandchildren in isolation from their parents, keeping them barred from each other. Grand Dukes Nicholas and Michael, the younger sons of Emperor Paul, complained that their mother was cold and estranged when they were small. Empress Maria, consort of Alexander II, failed to create a happy home, nor was Empress Maria Feodorovna reputed to be a concerned mother while Alexander III was still alive.

In the family of Emperor Nicholas efforts were made to keep all the children amiably close. They stayed with their mother in the evenings to play games and amuse themselves. Not a day passed without an opportunity to see her. All together they played forfeits, engaged in riddles, and the elder children and parents performed charades. The Tsar liked to sing chorus music with his children. Later we learn that childhood memories made a notable impact on the lifestyle at Maria's own court, and on the upbringing of her own children.

From very early on, Maria was involved in charitable work as was customary for people of her lineage. From 1835, she was a participating member of the Patriots' Society, which had been founded in the reign of Alexander I by his wife Empress Elizabeth Alexeyevna. The Society occasionally met in session in Maria's rooms at the Winter Palace. Special Sunday trade schools for girls were instituted by the members. In 1839, those schoolgirls earned a substantial amount of money — 9,000 roubles — for sewing the trousseau of Grand Duchess Maria.

13 G.DAWE, *Portrait of Grand Duke Alexander and Grand Duchess Maria,* children of Emperor Nicholas I, 1821. Gatchina, Palace-Museum.

Марiя
6го Декабря 1830 года

14, 15 **Sketch-book of Grand Duchess Maria.** 1826—30. The descendants of Grand Duchess Maria, who now live in the USA, have kept her childhood sketch-book with drawings dated 1826—30. Each drawing is signed, at first in child's scribble, later in beautiful handwriting. They are always dated, and there is sometimes an indication of where the work took place (26 July 1826, 1 March 1827, started in Peterhof in July 1830, Tsarskoye Selo, etc.). The progress of the novice artist is obvious. Her first shy attempts in mastering the geometric forms (a cube, a cylinder, etc) unfold into sketches of various types of trees: linden, maple, elm, common nut tree. Her final drawings (Maria was 10—11 years old) in pencil and watercolour were more sophisticated, depicting interiors, landscapes, ruins and castles, and intricate ornaments. (Eventually Maria Nikolayevna preferred to do watercolour painting. She occasionally presented her works to close friends. Architect Montferrand was said to assign a special room in his house on the Moika Embankment to exhibit a watercolour painting, a gift of Grand Duchess Maria). This sketch-book in worn out leather binding went through all the painful experiences together with the family: the revolution, wars, a cruel life as outcasts and refugees, an endless transfer through countries and continents. The surviving sketch-book is not a miracle, but testimony to high family morals. First publication.

16 T.A.NEFF, *Portrait of Grand Duchesses Maria and Olga.* Detail.
Grand Duchess Maria Nikolayevna.

17 T.A.NEFF, *Portrait of Grand Duchesses Maria and Olga,* 1838.
State Russian Museum, St. Petersburg.

18 V.I.HAUE, ***Grand Duchess Maria's room at the Winter Palace,*** before 1839.
State Russian Museum, St. Petersburg.

19 V.I.HAUE, ***Grand Duchess Maria's room*** at the Winter Palace. Detailed view of Maria's room.

20 UNKNOWN ARTIST. Detail of an untitled picture: Maria is easily recognized due to the similarity of her profile to that of her father.

21 UNKNOWN ARTIST, ***Untitled*** (Three Grand Duchesses in a room of the Winter Palace (?). Before 1839. The Romanov Family album. State Russian Museum, St. Petersburg. First publiction.

22 UNKNOWN ARTIST, *Nicholas I and his daughter Maria.* Detail.

23 UNKNOWN ARTIST, ***Emperor Nicholas I and his daughter Maria*** on the Neva Embankment, late 1820—30s. The Romanov Family album. State Russian Museum, St. Petersburg.

In her late teens, Maria was noted not only for her beauty and wit, but also for her strong will. In his memoirs 'My Past, My Thoughts' Alexander Hertsen tells a story about how Nicholas I tried to stare out Maria Nikolayevna. "She is much like her father, and her stare brings to mind his formidable gaze. His daughter courageously withstood that stare. He turned pale, his cheeks started trembling and there was more anger in his eyes; his daughter stared back in a similar manner. Everything around them began to pale and tremble, leib-freuleins and leib-generals were scared to breathe because of the cannibalistic duel of stares, similar to the one described by Byron in his 'Don Juan'. Nicholas got up, as he realized that it was a case of diamond cutting diamond".[3]

Her sister Olga, the future Queen of Württemberg, wrote in her girlhood diary that Maria was hot tempered, attentive and generous towards the poor, sympathetic to good deeds, but could not bear pretence or coercion. "She's a hundred times more virtuous than me, more dynamic than all seven of us, she lacks only a sense of duty".[4] Moreover, Maria was brave and inventive, appreciated novelty, and was almost indifferent to the opinion of high society. She was the first in the family to introduce skating as a routine pleasure for which everyone would travel by troika to the Tauride garden. In summer, she would skilfully slide down the 'montagne russe' which was erected in the largest hall of the Alexander Palace at Tsarskoye Selo.

The Empress worried about the future of her eldest daughter. Whom would she marry, bearing in mind her purity and sincerity, her ability to take a fancy, the instability of her emotions and yet, with such a lively wit and such numerous diverse talents? For her part, Maria firmly rejected any idea of marriage if it meant leaving Russia and changing her religion. Her parents' choice fell on Maximilian Duke of Leuchtenberg.

In 1837, the Bavarian King Louis commissioned his nephew Maximilian Joseph Eugen August Napoléon, Duke of Leuchtenberg (1817—52) to take part in the grand cavalry manoeuvres in Russia. He had sent a man who enjoyed the reputation in Europe as not only one of the most handsome men, but also one of the most educated and cultured princes.

24 K.P.BRIULLOV, *Portrait of Alexandra Feodorovna, wife of Nicholas I, and her daughter Maria Nikolayevna whilst riding in Peterhof Gardens,* 1837. State Russian Museum, St. Petersburg. This is a study from a gala portrait which was commissioned by Emperor Nicholas I to the celebrated painter Karlo Briullov, nicknamed Charles the Great by his contemporaries. It remained unfinished. The background shows the fountain statue 'Samson tearing apart the jaws of a lion' in the Lower Garden of Peterhof.

The House of the Dukes of Leuchtenberg was founded in 1817 by Eugène Rose de Beauharnais (1781—1824), son of Empress Joséphine by her first marriage, who was later adopted by his stepfather, Emperor Napoléon I in 1806. In 1805, His Imperial Highness, the Prince of France, Eugène de Beauharnais was installed by Napoléon I as Viceroy of Italy. In the following year he married Augusta Amalia, the eldest daughter of the King of Bavaria. After the restoration of the Bourbon dynasty, Eugène de Beauharnais had to leave Italy for Bavaria. King Maximilian I Joseph ceded the principality of Eichstätt to his son-in-law for five million francs, along with the title Duke of Leuchtenberg. Eugène, 1st Duke of Leuchtenberg, was also created Premier Hereditary Peer of Bavaria and lived in Munich where, in 1817—21, he built the Palais de Beauharnais for his huge family. It was designed by the famous architect Leo von Klenze. Eugène played no active role in politics until he died there in 1824 following a massive stroke. His widow commissioned a NeoClassical memorial from the sculptor Thorwaldsen which was erected in the west transept of St. Michael's in Munich.

25 **Palais de Leuchtenberg in Munich,** early 19C. The palace was built by Eugène de Beauharnais, 1st Duke of Leuchtenberg, in 1817—21 to the design of the architect Leo von Klenze. Sold by his descendants in the 1930s. In 1943, the palace was hit by a shell, but in 1945 it was heavily damaged during the American bombing raids. In 1957, the ruins became the property of the Federal Bavarian government. The decision was taken to dismantle the ruined structure and set up a new building after v.Klenze's design. During the restoration, workmen discovered several silver urns containing the hearts of the Leuchtenbergs which had once been immured in a recess of the family chapel. These were the hearts of Prince Eugène, his wife, and four of their children. The palace houses the Ministry of Finance of Bavaria at present.

26 ***Eugène de Beauharnais.*** Print of mid-19C, after J.Stieler. From the Munich collection of the Leuchtenbergs. Vicomte Eugène Rose de Beauharnais, a stepson of Emperor Napoléon I, enjoyed the latter's complete trust. The story has it that the dying Napoléon referred to him as he murmured: "Ah, Eugène! He is the one person in my family who never caused me any grief!".

27 **Memorial to Eugène de Beauharnais** in the west transept of St.Michael in Munich. The NeoClassical monument was commissioned by his widow Augusta Amalia, the daughter of King Maximilian of Bavaria, to the Danish sculptor B.Thorwaldsen. The figures of Clio, the Muse of History, and the two genii, who accompanied one from childhood to death, were executed by Pietro Tenerari. The Catholic church of St.Michael was badly damaged during the WW II air-raids by American bombers (1945). They have all been rebuilt.

28 F.GERARD, ***Portrait of Empress Joséphine,*** 1801.
State Hermitage, St. Petersburg.

29 V.V.VERE-SHCHAGIN, ***Fire in the Kremlin!,*** 1887—98. Present whereabouts unknown.

Maximilian, the youngest child and second son in the family of Eugène Beauharnais, lost his father as a little boy and was brought up by his enlightened mother. In 1835, after the death of his elder brother August Karl, the husband of the Queen of Portugal Maria II da Gloria, he became 3rd Duke of Leuchtenberg and entered the Bavarian military service. His elder sisters all made brilliant marriages. Joséphine married Oscar I, the King of Sweden and Norway, and from their marriage descend the present monarchs of Belgium, Denmark, Norway and Sweden, and the former Queen of the Hellenes and the Hereditary Prince of Luxembourg. Princess Amelie married Dom Pedro I, Emperor of Brazil; Princess Eugenie of Leuchtenberg married Friedrich Wilhelm, the last reigning Prince of Hohenzollern Hechingen, dying without issue; from Princess Theodolinde who married Wilhelm Alexander, the first Duke of Urach, Count of Württemberg, descended many of the most prestigious members of families of the Austrian and Italian nobility. Therefore, Eugène de Beauharnais is often nicknamed the 'grandfather of Europe', and Duke Maximilian and his descendants had relatives of prominence in many countries. It is not by chance that many grandchildren and great-grandchildren of Maria and Maximilian settled in these particular countries after 1917 and live there at the present time.

In October 1838, Max visited Petersburg again and made a good impression on the court with his handsome looks and knightly manner. It was exactly at this time that Olga noted in her diary: "In four days it has become clear that Max and Marie are made for one other".[5] The Duke was betrothed to the Tsar's favourite daughter. Paternal love and the desire to keep their child close to home prevailed. Her prospective marriage however met with some disapproval in Russia and also displeased many foreign courts, so thorough preparatory measures had to be taken.

In spring, engagement details were thrashed out by the parents visiting Germany: the Bavarian Catholic House was dismayed at the fact that Maximilian's children would by Russian law have to be baptized and brought up in the Orthodox faith. Max remained Catholic. Duchess Mother Augusta had a foreboding that the Leuchtenberg-Beauharnais family line, her dear Max being the last of the Leuchtenbergs, would die out if his descendants became native Russians. She said "history would blame her son".[6] But finally the marriage details were settled.

30 J.STIELER, ***Boy with a sabre,*** 1821. State Hermitage, St. Petersburg. Nationalized from the Leuchtenberg collection. Once attributed as a portrait of Alexander II as a child. Yet, in 1820—22, Joseph Stieler was commissioned to portray Eugène de Beauharnais, his wife and all their children. The date (1821) on it, and the age and appearance of the boy oblige us to ascertain that the sitter was Maximilian, the younger son, holding the favourite field sabre of his father Eugène de Beauharnais now belonging also to the Hermitage collection.

Before the official engagement ceremony on 5 December 1838 in Petersburg, Nicholas I and Maximilian visited Moscow where many tough characters refused to believe that the father of the betrothed was that very Eugène de Beauharnais, who had taken part in the fatal invasion by Napoléon's French army, which 26 years ago had left Moscow a devastated burning cinder. The Emperor impressed upon even the most obstinate Muscovites that they should regard Maximilian as his own fifth son.

The Bavarian archives of the Leuchtenbergs ascertain that, after the engagement, Prince P.M.Volkonsky, Minister of the Court and the Imperial Appanages, was ordered to provide Maria Nikolayevna with an annual allowance of 700,000 roubles from the Appanages; to pay her 2 million roubles and four per cent bonds immediately; to grant her a fully furnished palace in Petersburg with a court and a court-marshal, a fine country residence and everything else deserved by a grand duchess. Maria was also granted a court-meisterin and two ladies-in-waiting. Max, for his part, was granted two aides and an annual allowance of 100,000 roubles from the Appanages. However, it was reported to the Duchess Mother Augusta that these huge sums were not as substantial as they seemed, because court life in Petersburg was several times more expensive than that in London: ladies' outfits alone cost over 20,000 roubles a year, and all fashionable items had to be imported from abroad. The court personnel exceeded the size of any European court by five or six times, the staff distinguished more by rank and title than in their sense of responsibility.

On their engagement day, almost all Russian and Polish orders were conferred on Max, except for the orders of SS. George and Vladimir, which were the awards for outstanding service, and he was appointed Major-General in the Russian military, and honorary colonel of the Hussar Life Guards in Kiev. Thereafter he set off and for half a year was separated from his fiancée as he had to tend to land and property issues in his native Bavaria and Italy.

On July 2, 1839, the wedding took place at the Grand Church of the Winter Palace which had been newly restored after a fire. That ceremony was described in detail by the traveller, Marquis de Custine who visited St. Petersburg at that time. His book abounds in sarcastic resolute comments and negative impressions of Russia. The long and majestic Greek style wedding reminded him of the utmost fantasies from the 'One Thousand and One Nights'. "The church was packed to the brim with the envoys of all European and Asian monarchs... The Tsar's splendour seemed to rival God's own grandeur... now and then the Emperor left his place to move here and there in order to correct the errors of etiquette made by his children or the clergy". The Marquis notes how pure and graceful the bride was, how Maria and her sister Olga seemed to be the most beautiful women

31 ***Maximilian Duke of Leuchtenberg*** wearing a Hussar uniform, and parading in Palace Square, St. Petersburg. Private collection, USA. First publication.

in the church; how the groom lacked nobleness but was helped by his uniform which made him look somehow elegant, but that nevertheless he bore more resemblance to a lieutenant than to a duke, and above all, none of his relatives came to St. Petersburg. The Marquis then ends his story with the following words: “At the moment when the clergy and choir began to chant ‘We praise Our Lord’, guns fired to announce that the wedding was over. Words are not enough to describe the music, the gun fire, the ringing of the bells and the remote cries of joy of the people.”[7]

However, the Monarch was very annoyed that foreign princes did not attend Maria’s wedding. The marriage caused Prussian indisposition and the King delegated only a major Brauhitch to convey congratulations. Sweden alone sent her ambassador to wish happiness to the newly-weds.[8]

According to Paul Lacroix’s ‘History of Nicholas I’s Reign’, the Tsar presented his daughter with a huge malachite vase as a wedding gift, and Max received a fine sabre in good memory of his father-in-law, with the expressed wish that it never be used for other purpose. Lacroix describes the three rooms of the Winter Palace where Maria’s dowry was displayed: a hall with porcelain, crystal, silverware, table linen and other table accessories; another hall with gold and silver toilette items, exquisite underwear, lace, furs and various clothes. In the third hall was an exhibition of a dozen Russian style ceremonial outfits, wedding attire, Sunday dresses and festive wear, all of them accessorised with jewellery. There were necklaces and diadems of sapphire, emeralds, turquoise and rubies sparkling in the showcases. Max presented his wife with a necklace of six strings of impeccable pearls.

Never before had Petersburg witnessed such a glamorous wedding: the festivities lasted for two weeks, and sumptuous balls were announced. At the Winter Palace reception, ladies’ dresses surpassed all expectations in richness and elegance. Long beforehand, the Sovereign expressed his hope that the ladies of the court would disregard expenditure and make the ball miraculous. And indeed, no expense was spared as the ladies tried to outshine one another.

Colonel F.Hagern from the entourage of Prince Alexander of Orange, a cousin of Maria, son of the Queen of Netherlands and Grand Duchess Anna Pavlovna, who visited Petersburg immediately after the marriage, wrote of Grand Duchess Maria that she was small and much like her father in appearance and character. Her profile resembled that of young Catherine II. She was a gifted person, ‘a pearl in cotillion’, with a graceful figure and plenty of energy. Maria also demonstrated the will to rule. “From the first days of her married life she took the reins of governance into her hands”.[9]

32 *Maximilian Duke of Leuchtenberg.* Detail.

With his marriage Duke Maximilian was created Imperial Highness. Thus the prophecy of St. Savva came true. This spirited family legend

33 **Manifesto of Emperor Nicholas I,** dated 2 July 1839, and creating Maximilian Duke of Leuchtenberg His Imperial Highness, complimented with a new coat of arms, on his wedding day. First publication, by permission of Xenia v. Leuchtenberg USA. Front and back of the Manifesto, with the Imperial seal.

34 **Pages of the text of the Manifesto** stating the Imperial parents' happiness upon the marriage of Maria and Maximilian as blessed by God. Their hearts rejoiced at the Duke's decision to establish himself in Russia proving his love for his new parents-in-law and new Motherland. He was worthy of the title of His Imperial Highness and the new coat of arms.

БОЖІЕЮ
Поспѣшествующею Милостію
МЫ НИКОЛАЙ І^{Й}
ИМПЕРАТОРЪ
И САМОДЕРЖЕЦЪ ВСЕРОССІЙСКІЙ:
Московскій, Кіевскій, Владимірскій, Новгородскій,
ЦАРЬ Казанскій, ЦАРЬ Астраханскій, ЦАРЬ
Польскій, ЦАРЬ Сибирскій, ЦАРЬ Херсониса Таврическаго,
ГОСУДАРЬ ПСКОВСКІЙ И ВЕЛИКІЙ КНЯЗЬ
Смоленскій, Литовскій, Волынскій, Подольскій и Финляндскій,
КНЯЗЬ Эстляндскій, Лифляндскій, Курляндскій и Семигальскій,
Самогитскій, Бѣлостокскій, Корельскій, Тверскій,
Югорскій, Пермскій, Вятскій, Болгарскій и иныхъ,
ГОСУДАРЬ И ВЕЛИКІЙ КНЯЗЬ
Новагорода Низовскія земли, Черниговскій, Рязанскій,
Полоцкій, Ростовскій, Ярославскій, Бѣлозерскій,
Удорскій, Обдорскій, Кондійскій, Витебскій, Мстиславскій и всея
Сѣверныя страны Повелитель и Государь Иверскія, Карталинскія,
Грузинскія и Кабардинскія земли и Армянскія Области,
Черкасскихъ и Горскихъ Князей и иныхъ,
НАСЛѢДНЫЙ ГОСУДАРЬ И ОБЛАДАТЕЛЬ;
Наслѣдникъ Норвежскій, Герцогъ Шлезвигъ Голстинскій,
Стормарнскій, Дитмарсенскій и Ольденбургскій,
и прочая, и прочая, и прочая.

Манифестомъ Нашимъ во 2 день Іюля 1839 года даннымъ, изъявили Мы всенародно сколь радостенъ родительскому сердцу Нашему совершенный, при благословеніи Всемогущаго Промысла, счастный союзъ Любезной дочери Нашей Ея Императорскаго Высочества Великой Княгини Маріи Николаевны съ Герцогомъ Максимиліаномъ Лейхтенбергскимъ.
Вступивъ Герцогъ Лейхтенбергскій, къ утѣшенію Нашему и Любезнѣйшей Супруги Нашей Государыни Императрицы Александры Ѳеодоровны, намѣреніе основать пребываніе свое въ Россіи, оказывая привязанность Свою къ Намъ и Отечеству Нашему, даетъ Ему еще новыя права на любовь Нашу и уваженіе.
Въ ознаменованіе сихъ чувствъ Нашихъ, признали Мы за благо пожаловать Ему лично титулъ Императорскаго Высочества, со всѣми оному принадлежащими
Сею Грамотою присвояя и утверждая Ему сей Титулъ, Повелѣваемъ, дабы во всѣхъ актахъ, въ дѣлахъ публичныхъ и во всѣхъ отношеніяхъ частныхъ, на письмѣ и словесно симъ Титуломъ онъ всегда именовался, такъ какъ Мы онымъ Его пожаловали и наименовали, и

Гербъ соединяющій изображеніе Герба Императорскаго Нашего Дома съ Гербомъ Свѣтлѣйшаго Дома Лейхтенбергскаго установляемъ Ему нижеслѣдующій.
Черный двуглавый Орелъ увѣнчанный Императорскими Коронами, имѣетъ въ лапахъ: въ правой Скипетръ, а въ лѣвой Державу. На груди его большой съ Княжескою шапкою и цѣпью ордена Св. Апостола Андрея Первозваннаго щитъ, съ изображеніемъ прежняго Герба Его Императорскаго Высочества; онъ раздѣлясь на четыре части, имѣя сверхъ того въ срединѣ малый голубаго цвѣта щитъ съ Королевскою золотою Короною, въ первой и четвертой частяхъ означены въ серебреныхъ поляхъ горизонтально: въ первой голубая, въ четвертой чернаго цвѣта полоса, изъ коихъ надъ послѣднюю три черныя птицы, идущія по оной въ правую сторону; во второй въ красномъ полѣ крѣпостныя ворота и двѣ башни съ растущими на нихъ дубами, въ третьей части въ зеленомъ полѣ обращенный вверхъ остріемъ мечъ, имѣющій надъ рукоятью золотую шестиугольную звѣзду и около оконечности на каждой сторонѣ три такіяже звѣзды въ видѣ треугольниковъ

Во утвержденіе чего сію Грамоту собственноручнымъ подписаніемъ Нашимъ Мы утвердили и Государственною печатью укрѣпить повелѣли. Дана въ Санктпетербургѣ мѣсяца Декабря въ двадцать пятый день, въ Лѣто отъ Рождества Христова тысяча восемьсотъ тридцать девятое, Царствованія же Нашего въ пятоенадесять.
Николай
...запечатана въ Министерствѣ Иностранныхъ Дѣлъ № 11543.
Въ Сенатѣ въ книгу записана подъ № 1136.

among the Leuchtenbergs is still alive and has it that in 1812, Eugène de Beauharnais had rescued the Savva-Storozhev monastery from pillage at the closest approach to Moscow.That night Eugène had had a vision of an old bearded monk (St. Savva) who had predicted to him: "Take measures to protect my monastery from pillage and thus you shall survive, one of a few, to come back home safe and sound, and your offspring will serve Russia". And indeed, Eugène had returned safely to France, and remained one of few of the thousands to survive that perilous invasion. Almost 26 years later the second part of the prophecy came true.

On their wedding day the Tsar announced that the young couple should permanently reside at their own palace near St. Isaac's Square but until that time, they were given premises at the Corps de Pages in Sadovaya Street. In fact, the Winter Palace interior was still being rebuilt in 1839, but in the meantime the former Vorontsov Palace, an estate with many outbuildings which, from 1810 housed the most select military school, offered rare advantages. It was not only closely located to the Tsar's favourite Anichkov Palace with its large garden, but was also famous for its Maltese Catholic chapel as designed by the architect Giacomo Quarenghi. Maximilian was much moved by such a detail. One of their wedding gifts was Sergievka, a country estate bought from the Naryshkin family, located in a little bay opposite Kronstadt, which became much loved by all the Leuchtenbergs. Maria and Max spent their honeymoon there. They shut tight the gates which had always remained wide open to visitors under the Naryshkins.

Construction of the Maryinsky Palace

It was Emperor Nicholas I who chose the site and specified the design for his daughter's family residence as not a single private building in the centre of Petersburg, nor an office outside of the capital could be erected without his special permission. The Sovereign ordered the palace to be built on a site near the Blue Bridge on the left bank of the Moika river.

In the second half of the 18th century, that land had been occupied by the splendid house of Count Ivan G.Chernyshev, a well known statesman and diplomat in the reign of Catherine II. In 1762—68, the legendary palace with its fine interior and in all its splendour was built to the design of the Frenchman, Jean-B. Vallin de la Mothe. When in April 1768 the Count celebrated the house-warming, la Mothe presented the host with a set of prints of his new home drawn by Kolpashnikov.

Upon the death of Count Chernyshev, during the reign of Emperor Paul, Prince Conde lived in the house and noted the similarity of its interior in comparison with his own palace at Chantilly where he had once hosted the then Grand Duke Paul. Later on, Chernyshev's house was often leased out as offices, until in 1816, it was handed over to the Appanages department. Under Alexander I the building, being registered with the Military Collegium, was appointed to house the School of Guards Sub-Ensigns and Cavalry Junkers (in 1832—34 the poet Mikhail Lermontov studied there) which remained until 1838. The existing site was enlarged by the purchase of three nearby private houses in Noviy Lane, belonging to the Vulfert, Demut-Malinovsky and Savinkov families. In this way they aquired a huge parcel of free land along the Moika river embankment sandwiched between two streets.

Emperor Nicholas' order required his daughter's palace to be not only beautiful, surpassing other residences in grandeur, but also to be a comfortable home. The project had to incorporate top technical and engineering solutions of the day; to pioneer new ideas in layout and design; to use modern building materials to ensure durability and to cut construction costs. On top of all this, the overall design of the palace had to be in accordance with all the latest trends and the new artistic preferences of the epoch.

Фасадъ со стороны юга.

35 N.KOLPASHNIKOV, ***The Palace of Count Ivan Chernyshev on the Moika river embankment,*** late 1760s. Count Ivan G.Chernyshev (1726—97), a Fieldmarshal-General of the Navy and Chairman of the Admiralty Collegium at the end of his life, was a key figure in the reign of Empresses Elizabeth and Catherine II, and enjoyed much popularity with Grand Duke Paul. His diplomatic career in Vienna, Paris and London was quite a success.

36, 37 **The villa Sergievka of Maria Nikolayevna** (the Naryshkins' former manor in the country), rebuilt by Stakenschneider in 1839—42. Original drawings, Russian Academy of Art, St. Petersburg. First publication.

The late 1830s—40s marked a considerable decline of Classicism in Russian architecture, and as a new trend, Eclecticism began to develop. Eclecticism called for the application of a variety of different historical styles to the same building to enrich the design. Mixing styles of the past in the interiors was particularly admired as it produced a striking effect when moving from room to room. From then on, richness and virtuosity in decor detailing was considered to be the accomplishment to aim for.

In 1838, the draft project for Maria's palace was offered to Carlo Rossi, the most outstanding exponent of the Russian Empire style who created many monumental buildings and ensembles in St. Petersburg. At 63 years old, however, Rossi was too set in his ways to create the type of building then required. Thus, the Tsar entrusted the project to Andrey Stakenschneider (1802—65), a young and talented architect who had made himself well known by refurbishing several fine structures in St. Petersburg and on the outskirts. These included the ancient castle 'Fall' on an estate near Revel (Estland) which was redesigned in the new Gothic style for its owner, the omnipotent Count A.Ch.Benckendorf (1831); Prince Dolgoruky's villa on the Kamenny Island redecorated for Peter, Prince of Oldenburg, and a relative of the Tsar (1833); Nikolsky cottage in Peterhof for the Tsar's beloved consort (1835) among others. In 1834, Stakenschneider was awarded the title of 'Academician' of architecture and the rank of titular counsellor. The Sovereign showed much kindness to him. Incredible diligence, versatile knowledge and exquisite taste made him well known among his professional peers and popular with wealthy clients. By early 1839, he was already a 9th class Academician, had been awarded the order of S.Stanislaus and employed as the Court architect of HIH Grand Duke Michael Pavlovich, head of three key departments in the Russian Empire and the younger brother of the Tsar.

Andrey Stakenschneider, the grandson of a German tanner who had been commissioned into service by Emperor Paul I, was born at his father Johann's mill. He eventually mounted the architectural Olympus because of his efficiency and talent and never stepped down once, right up to his sudden death in 1865. The Romanovs made him the privileged designer of the royal and grand ducal palaces. Yet, with no less brilliance he built private homes, churches, chapels, railway stations and hospitals, bridges and barracks which always required special knowledge. By the end of his life, he was appointed Chief Architect to the Appanages department and His Imperial Majesty's Own Palace.

38 I.A.HOCH, ***Portrait of the architect Andrey Stakenschneider,*** 1860.
State Hermitage, St. Petersburg.

The Maryinsky Palace was his first really important commission in St. Petersburg which set him on the path to fame and success. In creating this palace Stakenschneider acted as an architect of the transitional epoch, willingly employing Classical tradition and using the new trends of the day in his own creative way.

His talent and erudition never failed. His capacity for work was prodigious: throughout the five years he was supervising construction on the Moika river site, he was simultaniously engaged in building several palaces and villas for other members of the Imperial family on the southern coast of the Gulf of Finland, around Peterhof and between Strelna and Peterhof. We shall name just a few of them.

In 1839—42, at the Sergievka estate (west of Peterhof), on Maria's orders, Stakenschneider rebuilt the Naryshkins' old country house and set up instead a magnificent summer palace in the style of a Roman patrician villa. Almost simultaneously he supervised the construction of two Pompeian style pavilions on the Tsaritsa and Olga Islands in Peterhof, the Pavilion and Church at Babygon, whilst redesigning in the new Gothic style the dining-room at the Cottage in Peterhof. Work was in full swing on the construction of the NeoBaroque private dacha for the Crown Prince Alexander, on the site of the obsolete mansion which, in the 1770s, Yuri Felten had once built in Old Peterhof near Sergievka.

The initial design of the residence on the Moika site was taken for His Majesty's approval immediately after the engagement of Max and Maria had taken place. An order from the Tsar dated March 1st 1839 to Prince P.M.Volkonsky, Minister of the Imperial Court and Appanages stated that the construction was to be supervised by the architect Stakenschneider in person and that the required money should be allotted by the Appanages. The construction cost was estimated at only 700,000 roubles, although very expensive materials such as marble, zinc, and cast iron were to be employed. In comparison, we should note that the previous account submitted by Rossi to the Appanages in 1819 for the construction of Grand Duke Michael's Palace amounted to 6 million roubles. Labour and materials remained cheap in Stakenschneider's day, yet, construction costs were cut further because of the use of prefabricated metal members, and some of the earlier basement and walls were kept: the former Chernyshev house was not levelled, but it was incorporated into the new buildlng in accordance with usual practice. Three of the old walls were so solid and proved so obstinate that Stakenschneider had to adjust his project to them.

The site was cleared in summer 1839, and the official foundation ceremony took place on October 1, 1839. Works proceeded at a fast pace,

39 ARNU, Sr,
Palace of the Duke of Leuchtenberg,
c.mid-19C. Institute of Russian Literature, St. Petersburg.

so that by the end of 1840 the building work was almost finished except for two side pediments and the central attic floor. The crucial construction project was coordinated by a committee of which the architects Carlo Rossi and Vasili Stassov were members.

By carefully placing the building on an asymmetrical land site between two streets, Stakenschneider succeeded in including the palace in an almost completed architectural ensemble of St. Isaac's Square, the dominant feature of which was the half-finished St. Isaac's Cathedral (1818—58, arch. Auguste Montferrand). The plans show the palace as being uncommonly asymmetrical: its right wing of nearly 24 m is not only much shorter than its left wing of nearly 56 m, but is also at an oblique angle towards the main façade due to the line of Voznessensky Avenue.

To an ordinary Petersburg dweller the swift growth of the Maryinsky just opposite St. Isaac's still under construction must have seemed fantastic, a kind of construction miracle, as the newspapers of the day proclaimed.

Provincial gentlemen and inhabitants of remote suburbs who had not visited St. Isaac's Square for a couple of years were astonished: in less than a year and a half a monumental residence appeared with an amazing façade of over 100 m, and three floors reaching nearly 20 m in hight. In fact, the earlier famous grand ducal Marble and Michael Palaces are U-shaped and the length of their façades is less significant.

In 1842—44, the Blue Bridge in front of the palace was widened from 41 m to 97.3 m to match the front façade of the Maryinsky, and thus, the building seemed even more to be an integral part of the square. On gaining such a wide approach and grand view the palace was second to none, except the Winter Palace of the Emperor himself.

The front façade of the Maria Palace features "traditional principles of Russian Classicism: its central section and flanks are set slightly forward, the ground floor is accentuated in 'diamond' rustication, and the two upper storeys are lined with Corinthian columns and pilasters",[11] wrote Professor Andrey Punin of Petersburg, an author of many books on the history of architecture. The Classical motif in the design was necessitated by the altogether Classical ensemble of St. Isaac's Square with St.Isaac's Cathedral, the houses of Prince Lobanov-Rostovsky (arch. A.Montferrand, 1817—20), and those of the Miatlev family (arch. A.Rinaldi, 1760s, formerly the Naryshkins' house). From the Maryinsky site, the view opened out onto the Classical Cavalry Academy (arch. J. Quarenghi, 1804—07) and the Empire style façades of the Senate and Synod (arch. C. Rossi, 1829—34). The Maryinsky enclosed the south side of the square and was described as the 'Roman palace' by sophisticated locals. Soon, in 1844—53, the ensemble was

40 **View from the palace balcony.** St. Isaac's Cathedral and the square in front of it.

41 Maryinsky Palace as seen from the Blue Bridge.

42 The main (northern) façade of the palace.

43 **The central portico** with two ramps on the northern façade served as the main entrance into the Maryinsky Palace. Antique fashion standard lamps frame the side arches.

complete with the building of the office of the Ministry of State Property and the house of its minister on the east and west sides of the square according to the designs of the architect Nicholas Yefimov.

The central section has a high attic storey which gives an impressive Imperial feel to the façade. The attic front is decorated with six strong vertical volutes and ornamentation in relief between them, with a copper double headed eagle in the central niche, an indispensable decoration, inside or outside, in all the palaces of the Tsar's children — Constantine, Maria and Nicholas. An imposing main entrance has a projecting portico with wide central steps and two sweeping side ramps. Antique style standard lamps frame the side arches. Above the portico, on the first floor level, there is a wide balcony with a decorative balustrade and six cast iron vases covered in stucco to match the façade.

Newly fashionable yellow-grey sandstone was used for decorative elements on the front façade along with details cast in English cement. This kind of sandstone was excavated in Estland at the Bistrom quarries, and brought to St. Petersburg by water, down the Luga river and along the Gulf of Finland. It is worth mentioning that many construction materials had to be brought from far away places.

Contemporaries of Stakenschneider appreciated his technical skills in particular, for he took into account the restoration experience of the Winter Palace and made extensive use of the fireproof construction elements such as metal overhead covers upon metal struts and bars. Metal mesh in ceilings to support the plaster for durability and light ceramic components in vaults were among the technical novelties. Reports of the day spoke proudly of new technical feats not yet practiced even in France, the then accepted leader in architectural technology. Fire resistance was of overriding concern to the Emperor, and specific attention was paid to this matter in the design. The rage and fear of Nicholas I had yet to subside following the sudden and awful fire which destroyed the Winter Palace in December, 1837. For three days that fire had raged through the palace, and the Tsar and his brother Grand Duke Michael had personally taken part in efforts to quench the flames. Hence, in 1845 reports of the Maryinsky emphasized that everything in the palace was made of stone and metal, except for the floors.

Stakenschneider also came up with a brilliant solution to his client's other requirement — that of creating a home of the utmost comfort. He situated the service and the guest rooms facing out onto the street, whilst the living rooms were placed inside the building, away from the noise of rattling carriages and street peddlars' calls. And yet, the private rooms remained well lit and sunny as they looked out onto inner yards and a spacious south-facing garden. The layout of several hundred rooms in the palace

44 **Balcony with a decorative balustrade** and Italianate cast iron vases with lids, covered in stucco to match the façade.

was skilfully adjusted to meet practical problems: enfilades were complemented by nearby passages; ceremonial suites were close to private rooms. The staircases were well positioned, and their artistic and technical flair were to become the architect's particular success.

A unique ramp was designed and installed in the right wing, connecting all three floors away from the main rooms. The ramp was used for wheelchairs and prams, and for walking up and down to 'avoid shortness of breath'. The oval ramp space receives natural light through a skylight in the ceiling. The struts, banisters and rails are constructed in cast iron, the slopes are coated with parquet flooring, although records mention that they were originally covered in asphalt. The ramp enjoyed great popularity among the inhabitants, its entrance hall doors led out to the square, the garden and into the ground floor main passage. People used the ramp to get to the palace church on the attic floor.

The colossal indoor ramp was unique in a private residence in Petersburg in the 19th century. It is no coincidence that in reports of 1845, 1865, and 1885, the ramp is mentioned as a unique fantastic construction in the capital. Not long after, hydraulic and pneumatic lifts were introduced, the prototype of modern lifts. Stakenschneider's next design (the Grand Duke Nicholas' Palace for Maria's brother), approved by the Emperor in 1853, envisaged a mahogany lift.

Outside, the garden south frontage was provided with an additional ramp reaching up to first floor level. "...a wide alley runs through the garden towards the private entrances to allow carriages to approach. One of the entrances is furnished with a ramp reaching to the

45 **The Ramp.** A cross-section, 1845.

46 **The indoor Ramp.** The unique design of a staircase without steps in a private residence, connecting all three floors away from the main rooms.

47 **Small Corner Study** of the Grand Duchess with an entrance onto the balcony furnished with an additional ramp reaching up to first floor level. A light coach could approach it directly.

first floor, thus allowing a light coach to come straight to it", a witness wrote in 1845 in the 'St. Petersburg Chronicle (Vedomosti)'.[12] In an archive record titled 'Exterior Ramp description' (1845) it was noted that roofing iron, granite plates, lead, and waxed felt were used to build the upper landing; the slope was carefully walled up, and a guard's room was installed at its foot. Although the exterior ramp was dismantled after the Grand Duchess died, it can be still traced.

Both ramps confirm evidence of the direct participation of the royal client in designing the palace. Maria reminded her Court Minister that a lift was a must, but she received the most unusual engineer's solution to her request in the form of the ramp. Hearsay has it that, Maria Nikolayevna complained about leg pains which had grown worse after her first childbirths, and which worsened still further towards the end of her life. Any sort of illness in the Imperial family was kept very quiet. Undoubtedly

Stakenschneider was urged by his clients to come up with solutions to protect the secret illness of the young hostess, and the ramp remained a unique feature unknown to thousands of homes in St. Petersburg.

In return for his technical achievements on this project, for his creative endeavour and unmatched comprehension of architecture Stakenschneider was appointed Professor of the Art Academy, even before his plans had been fulfilled as a designer of great renown.

Work on the interior was completed by the end of 1844. For over four years the Duke of Leuchtenberg personally supervised construction. He wanted his new home to be not only a comfortable and beautiful family hearth, but also a place to work and to see people who came to call on business.

On 25 January 1845, the palace was approved by a special commission and inaugurated. By special Imperial Decree it was handed over to the Sovereign's daughter and named Maryinsky after her. However, the family did not move in immediately.

"In early 1845, the Maryinsky Palace was opened to the curious public", wrote Nestor Kukolnik, one of the first visitors. "Rooms thronged with

48 **The southern façade of the palace, and the garden** with fountains, alleys and pathways. Photo, late 19C.

crowds".[13] Reports of the day praised the elegance and originality of the interior. Contemporaries appreciated the Emperor's generosity in lavishing money on his favourite daughter to create a magic castle as the capital's latest palace was immediately christened.

A reader today can hardly imagine a crowd of commoners in the royal suites, and the sheer idea of it seems improbable. And yet, from the time of Empress Elizabeth who adored all kinds of festivities it was traditional to organise a populous masquerade on January 1, at the Winter Palace. "By the appointed hour all the Palace was illuminated, and the doors thrown open. Everyone was welcome. The first guest to come and the last to leave were recorded... (under Alexander I). More than 30,000 guests of all shapes and sorts would attend. Needless to say, there were no security measures",[14] writes Count Vladimir Sollogub. Balls at the Winter Palace were also held under Nicholas I: "In 1828, on January 1, a ball complete with mouzhiks (commoners) took place... Each was counted by the police and then allowed in, but no more than 40,000 were permitted... they could stay until midnight".[15] These are lines from the memoirs of Alexandra Smirnova (Rossette), a friend of both Pushkin and Gogol. According to Baroness Maria Frederycksz, 30,000 tickets were issued for the masquerade on January 1, 1837. In 'The Russian Journal of Lady Londonderry, 1836—37', the English visitor mentions the great ball on New Year's day in 1836: "The whole of the Hermitage and Winter Palace are thrown open and lighted up and crowds of the commonest and dirtiest people admitted. More than forty thousand tickets are issued, and coachmen, servants and mouzhiks, etc. are all allowed to enter, walk about and take refreshment... not a case of drunkenness or dishonesty. Though all the treasures of the palace are left open, not a bit of plate is ever missed".[16] Therefore, the Grand Duchess Maria, in her own way, observed the tradition to give pleasure to the most simple person as she had been brought up to do from childhood.

The Maryinsky Palace became the last huge construction in St. Petersburg. For 40 years the building remained the family hearth of the Romanov-Leuchtenbergs in the form as completed by Stakenschneider. Alterations were minimal and at the wish of the owners; the almost finished gala dining-room was turned into a part of the guest room suites; later, a wing for the

49 H.VERNET, ***Carousel (Roundabout) at Tsarskoye Selo,*** 1843. The Catherine Palace, Tsarskoye Selo Museum-Reserve. Equestrian costumed tournament (carousel) echoed the medieval tournament tradition in later periods. As ordered by Nicholas I, such a tournament took place on 23 May 1842, at the Alexander Garden in Tsarskoye Selo. Participants were 16 men wearing medieval armour and ladies in medieval outfits. On the left of the Imperial couple one can see Crown Prince Alexander and Duke Maximilian dressed as knights, Constantine, Nicholas and Michael, the three younger sons, were portrayed as costumed pages. Olga and Alexandra boasted gorgeous finery of brocade and velvet. The oldest daughter Maria was not in the group as she was entertaining the guests with ice-cream and tea at the colonnade of the Alexander Palace.

50 H.VERNET, ***Carousel at Tsarskoye Selo.*** Detailed representation from the autocrat couple. Nicholas I as a knight was wearing authentic armour of the 16th century, in the day of King Maximilian of Germany, a matter of particular pride in the Tsar's arms collection. The focal point was Empress Alexandra wearing a splendid medieval costume, symbolizing a happy mother and a beautiful lady worthy of worship, inspirational to a man in combat.

children was added in the courtyard, and some changes took place to the church on the attic floor. Only in 1867—68, were rooms in the east wing refurbished by the architect Ippolito A.Monighetti to accomodate the grown up sons, the Dukes of Leuchtenberg.

Whlist the Maryinsky Palace remained under construction, three children were born in the family of Maria and Max. In summer they usually lived in Gatchina and Tsarskoye Selo, the traditional sites for the Tsar's hunt and marvellous festivities. Thus, in May 1842 Emperor Nicholas I ordered a memorable costumed carousel in the Alexander park of Tsarskoye Selo. All resplendent Petersburg attended the equestrian tournament. Horace Vernet, the eminent French painter, who that year was invited to work in Russia immortalized the event by portraying the main participant riders. The family portrait pleased the monarch very much. He decorated Vernet with the order of Alexander Nevsky and presented him with a carriage complemented by a coachman and horses. From that time on, Vernet was seen in Paris riding in a Russian style vehicle.

Maria's Family Home

So, Maria's family celebrated their housewarming. What was life like in their new home? Memoirs of those days, the meticulously kept German and scanty Russian archives containing private correspondence and diaries of the former owners of the palace, the old newspaper and magazine articles and gossip columns help to tune into the 'rustles of history', as the poet Alexander Blok put it, and to sense the aura of the Golden Age of Russian culture.

51 **Main façade of the Maryinsky Palace at night.**

A visitor to the new palace where the young family had finally settled was immediately impressed with the resplendent spacious ENTRANCE HALL. There were columns and pilasters of pink Tivdian marble from Karelia, a fireplace of green Siberian marble, and a granite tiled floor with a herring-bone pattern. The light arcade was painted with arabesques. The colossal scale and fine decoration of Russian hallways, always a specific point of concern for any architect, strikes the foreigner with wonder. When balls and receptions were taking place above, this space was filled for hours with hundreds of sleepy servants and lackeys enveloped in sheepskins and Siberian skin-coats, each carefully nursing his mistress's costly fur. In the daytime, less important people used to leave their topcoats there.

52 **The Entrance Hall** features columns and pilasters of pink Tivdian marble from Finland. In 1885 it was redecorated in order to use the Maryinsky Palace for governmental offices, and has remained an administrative building ever since.

To the left of this area is the wide steep GRAND STAIRCASE in the restrained surrounding of white scagliola walls, with detailed mouldings and richly punctuated ceiling and coving, and medallion paintings. It was adorned with the niched gesso statues of ancient warriors in its lower part, whilst seven wall brackets supported the busts of Trojan war heroes. The busts are believed to depict Paris and the three goddesses who claimed the golden apple of discord, and later protected both the Greeks and the Trojans. Marble lionesses on metal plinths guarded the base of the main staircase, flanked on either side by two ormolu lamps. Directly above the first steps are the letters spelling out Maria's full name in the form of an intricate stucco gilded motif which is set close to a narrow multifigure moulded frieze in NeoGreek style.

53 **View from the Entrance Hall up onto the Grand Staircase.**

54 **The main Staircase,** which rises to a half landing and then continues in two stairways up to the first floor, has seven landings laid in grey and white marble plates. View from the half landing down onto the Entrance Hall and up, towards the ceremonial enfilade. Classical chaste decor imbues the stairwell with dignified severity.

55 **Niched gesso statue** of an ancient warrior at the Staircase landing.

56 **Detailed moulded motif** spelling out Maria's name is set above the staircase portal. This gilded ornamentation is used throughout the palace.

57 **The open wrought-iron balustrade** has mahogany banisters and rich gilding. The original dark green paint had been covered with other subsequent paints and was only uncovered during the restoration works carried out in the 1970s.

58 **One of the marble lioness** figures at the base of the Stairway which were removed after 1945. Photo, 1940.

59 **The Grand Staircase** in the late 19C.

60 **An ormolu torchère** at the Stairway base. In the old days, a marble lion sculpture was placed on the plinth.

61, 62 **The Grand Staircase** has the elaborate ceiling and coving painted en grisaille, and depicting ancient warriors in medallions. Seven wall brackets support the busts of Trojan war heroes.

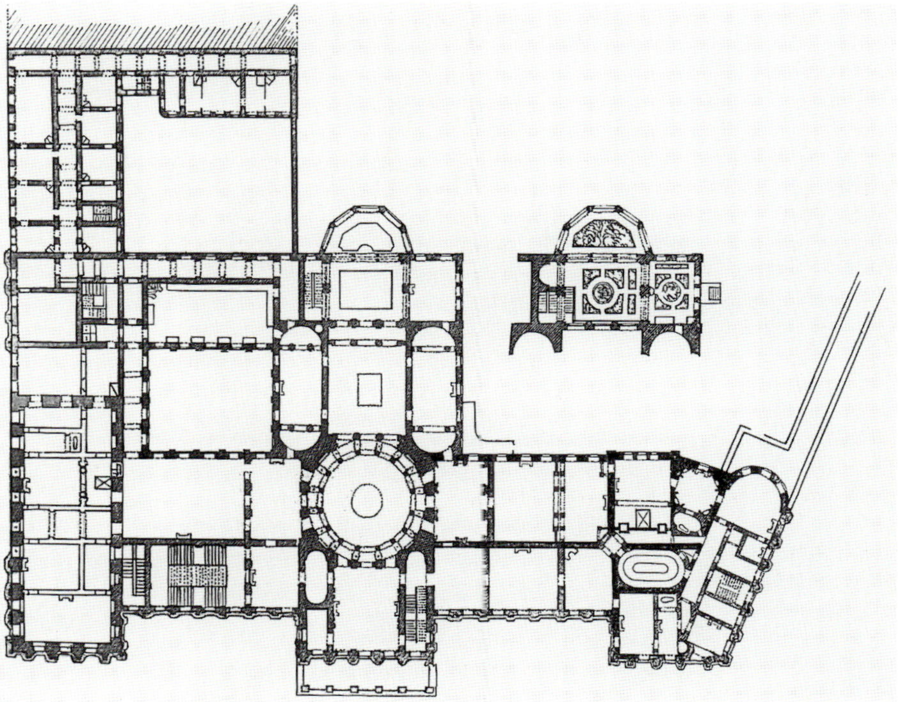

63 **Old first floor plan,** 1845.

On the first floor above the hallway was the GALA RECEPTION ROOM, looking out onto the square, with an entrance onto the balcony. An enfilade of main halls commenced from this room designed in the rather traditional Russian Classical style. This spacious room with windows in two rows is splendid, in spite of the restrained decor and moderate gilding. Nine huge bas-reliefs above the cornice feature episodes from Homer's 'Iliad' after the design of the eminent English NeoClassical sculptor John Flaxman (1755—1826). These alternate with eight enormous altoreliefs of ancient armour. The high refined ceiling of modest colouring and gilding is plaster on a metal mesh, and was the first example of its kind on such a scale.

65 **Charity bazaar in the Reception Room** in 1877. Drawing, late 19C.

64 **The Gala Reception Room** is located on the northern façade of the palace. However, daylight pours in through the double row of huge windows and makes the room wonderfully bright. Three French doors lead onto a balcony.

Dark red marble pilasters which were chosen to echo the colours of the red granite colonnade of St. Isaac's across the square provide a fine contrast to the elaborate white Carrara marble fireplaces. The carved friezes on the fireplace feature idyllic scenes from peasant life, while the side pilasters in relief are shaped into perfectly detailed trees. On one side there is a bird in the tree, on the other the bird is sitting in its nest to symbolize that Maria had now started a family. The rather German feel of the design is attributed to the influence of Empress Alexandra Feodorovna, who was Princess Charlotte of Prussia by birth.

Seven exquisite doors of polished rosewood inlaid with ivory, mother-of-pearl and copper arabesques are the highlight of the room. The design reveals ancient characters in medallions, mythical beings driving chariots, each one of which is pulled by a different animal, including harnessed horses, lions, deer, swans and peacocks. The main panels feature gods and goddesses in billowing pink and blue robes, chieftains with clubs sitting in a chariot, helmeted warriors with swords, with all the scenes elaborately surrounded by floral arabesques. The door handle is an ormolu bird's claw tightly holding a wooden miniature globe. Later, Stakenschneider also used this handle design on the doors of the Grand Duke Nicholas' Palace. It also became popular as a motif in jewellry. There are seven doors in all; three of them were commissioned in Munich in 1842, the others were made to match by Russian craftsmen. The inlaid parquet floor is unequalled in the palace in its variable pattern and the selection of costly wood.

66 **The Gala Reception Room** commences a ceremonial enfilade which Stakenschneider extended back into the palace. From the Reception Room three doors lead into the Rotunda, the Square Room and the Winter Garden gallery at the far end of the enfilade. The doors of this room are considered to be the most splendid in the palace.

Originally the focal point of the room was a large agate vase over 1 m in height on a porphyry plinth. It was made at the Kolyvan works in the Urals. Above it, one could see the top of the water fountain in the Winter Garden on the far side of the Rotunda, the Square room and also the garden gallery. These four premises form an enfilade which extends back into the building, a feature rarely found in the 19th century, but fashioned after the enfilade of the Tauride Palace as designed by the architect Ivan Starov in the late 18th century.

67 **Elaborately coffered ceiling** is delicately picked out with paint and gold. It is one of the earliest examples in Russia of plaster on a metal mesh of such a large scale. Nine bas-reliefs above the cornice form a broad frieze around the room and feature episodes from Homer's 'Iliad'.

69 **Impressive door of polished rosewood,** inlaid with engraved ivory, tinted mother-of-pearl and copper arabesques. The panel design reveals female half-figures, warriors, ancient characters, lions, as well as floral ornamentation with griffins, birds and tritons. The door handle is an ormolu bird's claw (1842) tightly holding a wooden ball

70 **Detail of a central door panel** inlaid in mother-of-pearl, and featuring gods and goddesses driving chariots each one of which is pulled by harnessed lions, horses, deer, swans and peacocks.

71 **Seven sumptuous doors** of rosewood decorate the Gala Reception Room. Three of them were commissioned in Munich in 1842, the others were made to match by Russian craftsmen.

72 **The central French window** with an entrance onto the balcony framed by paired fluted marble pilasters.

73 **Carved gilded curtain rail** with elements of ancient decor.

74 **The Reception Room** looks onto St. Isaac's Cathedral and the square in front of it. Dark red marble pilasters here were chosen to echo the colours of the red granite colonnade of St. Isaac's.

76 **The fanciful floor design** in the Gala Reception Room is inlaid mainly in oakwood and other precious wood. The central part has a herring-bone pattern with a wonderful rosette in the middle. It is accompanied by the broad border of oblique checker marquetry, and the outer border of acanthus leaves and palmettos.

75 **Detail of the inlaid border** in the Gala Reception Room.

77 **Fireplace** in the Gala Reception Room. Dark raspberry marble of the wall ornation and opulent rosewood doors provide a fine contrast to two exquisite white Carrara marble fireplaces.

78 **Detailed frieze** of a fireplace. Bas-relief features a youth talking to an old man surrounded by children, against the idyllic landscape background.

79 **Detail of an intricate fireplace carving.** The side pilasters in relief are shaped into perfectly detailed trees, with a bird in the tree on the right pilaster. On the left, the bird is sitting in its nest to symbolize that Maria had now started a family.

The ROTUNDA, a round hall of amazing proportions, reaches up 17 m into a huge cupola skylight. Elegant ormolu chandeliers hang between 32 columns which encircle the hall in two tiers and evoke a festive and triumphant mood. The ceiling, with moulded decoration against gilded background, is unusual in its structure: the stone dome rests on the walls at only four points. The overall effect is lightness and refinement due to the open ironwork of the gallery and the frieze above the first row of columns, which has a design of pairs of gilded griffins, each pair holding a lyre. When the guests assembled and musicians played from the height of the lace-like gallery, the Rotunda was beyond comparison. A rosette of costly wood can be seen in the middle of the beautifully inlaid floor.

80 **The Rotunda** is a crossing of the two enfilades which run parallel and perpendicular to the main façade. The view from the Gala Reception Room onto the Rotunda and further onto the Square Room. The elaborate floor design with a fine circular border and central marquetry rosette.

81 **Charity bazaar** in the Rotunda in 1877.
Drawing, late 19C.

82 **Thirty two fluted Corinthian columns** encircle the hall in two tiers.
During grand receptions and private concerts musicians played from the higher tier.

83 **Huge cupola skylight,** 17m high. Magnificent ornate ceiling has coffers in two circles, highlighted with moulding and gilding.

84 **The lower Corinthian colonnade** with crystal ormolu chandeliers
and the richly ornate frieze at second floor level, forms a passage into the Square Room.

85 **Rotunda.** The metal balustrade is highlighted with bright gold. The frieze over the capitels shows elaborate moulding with a design of gilded griffins, each pair holding a lyre.

The old plan of the first floor shows that the Rotunda is a crossing of the two enfilades which run parallel and perpendicular to the main façade.

86 **Doors on the left of the Rotunda** led into the private apartments of Maria Nikolayevna and Duke Maximilian.

87 **Rotunda.** "...elegant, as everything erected by my father", wrote Helen Stakenschneider in her memoirs.

The Rotunda continues into the SQUARE ROOM (also called Pompeian Room), an area again lighted through a glass skylight. Two walls are formed into double tier galleries with columns which give the space a light and airy feel. Ornamentation is in Pompeian style, imitating the mural decorative painting which had been uncovered by archaeologists in ruins of the ancient Roman period, particularly at the Pompeii excavation site. That ornamental painting depicted a typical motif of intertwining plant forms, scrolls, masks, mythical characters, animals and architectural designs. The decorative surrounds to the square and rectangular wall panels are painted in Grotesque style. The murals, the coffered ceiling with gold touches are richly painted in tempera on plaster by Drollinger, who also did the landscape painting above the doorways styled after ancient frescoes. The wall medallions in oil on canvas are also by Drollinger. Four grand torchères of bronze and porcelain, made at the Alexander Imperial porcelain works after a Stakenschneider drawing, originally stood in the corners of the room. Those torchères immediately became the highlight of the capital. In 1865, they still attracted much attention in the 'Illustrated Newspaper' column when the Maryinsky Palace interior was described.

89 **A view of the Square Room,** or Pompeian Hall. Brightly painted caissoned ceiling has nine coffers, of which the central one is used as a glass skylight. Mural painting on both levels is in rich arabesque patterns.

88 **A torchère of porcelain and ormolu** from the Square Room. Drawing, 1845. Four torchères were made at the Alexander Imperial porcelain works after a Stakenschneider drawing. They immediately became the highlight of St. Petersburg.

90 Walls painted with murals in Pompeian style became a popular motif in Russia in the mid-19C. The top mural decor was badly damaged during the siege of Leningrad by leakages causing damp spots, paint decay, and holes in the painted cloth.

91 **Two walls of the Square Room** are shaped as open galleries with columns which give the space a light and airy feel.

92 Each wall is divided into three ornate panels. Wall panel surrounds were painted in tempera on plaster by Drollinger who was also responsible for the wall medallions in oil on cloth.

93 **A huge ormolu chandelier** hangs in the centre of the Square Room. Made in St. Petersburg after a Stakenschneider drawing.

94 **Detail of the fresco decor** above the door.

95 **A corner of the Square Room** decorated with paired Corinthian pilasters. Wall panels feature cherubs, mythical characters, sphinxes, birds and animals in Grotesque style, as well as meander bands and plant forms.

96 ***Grand Duchess Maria* in her Winter Garden** (painted by T.Neff.
The picture was inherited by George Nikolayevich, Maria's grandson).

97 **The Winter Garden.** Drawing, mid-19C.

Three pairs of doors led from the Square Room to the gallery of the three-storey WINTER GARDEN. Its upper part had walls, columns and pilasters faced in scagliola, and a richly painted ceiling featured a huge skylight of 680 framed panes. The lower part of the garden consisted of numerous grottoes and cascades with a central fountain spurting a jet of water about 8 m into the air. Another fountain of droplets, made out of shells was also in action. It was called the 'Fountain of Tears' and was styled after the Bakhchisarai fountain in the Crimea which became the prototype for the fountains in the Pavilion Hall of the Small Hermitage. In this spacious garden were arched pillars and 8 columns. An attractive exit into the outdoor garden had a porch with posts and 5 granite steps. Palm trees and other exotic plants grew in 30 marble flower boxes along the pathways laid with marble mosaics. Up in the gallery, among the unusual plants, birds chirruped and preened themselves. The garden received abundant daylight through its 24 windows and the skylight, containing over 1,000 glass panels in all, and at night it was brightly lit up. Anna Tiutcheva, a lady-in-waiting received by the Grand Duchess Maria in her garden in 1853, described it as "A real mirage of spring amidst the January frost".[18]

To the east of the Square Room is the CONCERT HALL (or BALL ROOM). The hall has two rows of windows facing the inner yard. Its walls are covered with creamy scagliola and divided into smooth panels with antique decorative surrounds and gesso ornaments enhanced with gold detailing in the corners. Moulded gilded lyres sit between the windows in the upper tier.

The room was famous for a deep sculptured frieze featuring paintings on the theme of Mars and Venus. The formidable Mars, embodiment of the horrors of war, could only be defeated by Venus, the Goddess of Beauty. Their union gave birth to a daughter Harmonia and a son Eros (Cupid or Love). The union of War and Love, Power and Beauty attracted and pleased the clients. We soon learn that Maria was rather fascinated by the goddess Venus as the Venus motif is often encountered in the decor of her private rooms. These scenes in the frieze were painted by Antonio Vighi. He had been invited by the architect V. Brenna to work on the Michael Castle, but he stayed on, and after 40 years had decorated virtually all the superior rooms in the palaces and villas of the Petersburg élite, both inside and outside the capital. The skilful brush of the elderly master was never idle for long. The painting in the frieze was his last commission. The artist died whilst working on it at 81 years of age, without even receiving his fee.

98 **The Concert Hall.** Its coffered ceiling of exquisite design is astonishing in rich moulding and painting, and is highlighted with gold. Crystal chandeliers were made at the Imperial glass factory for this hall after a Stakenschneider drawing.

99 **Detail of the Concert Hall** interior with a chandelier. Photo, 1940.

100 **A sculptured frieze** featuring paintings on Greek mythology which was executed by Antonio Vighi. Photo, 1940.

The ceiling of the Concert Hall is moulded, beautifully coffered and highlighted with gold. It is further evidence of the varied and inimitable motifs which Stakenschneider used to design the Maryinsky ceremonial rooms. Unfortunately the original marble fireplace, with its two caryatids holding musical instruments, was dismantled in 1945—46 when resto-

101 **The Concert Hall** was adorned with the Imperial family portraits, late 19C.

ration works began after the destruction caused by the siege of Leningrad, and the caryatids were replaced with two plain columns.

Magnificent huge conical chandeliers, with 8 matching wall lights, were specially made in 1842 in the Imperial glass factory. Small cosy chairs with small cushions, commissioned from the cabinetmaker Andrey Tur, lined the walls.

102 **The fireplace decorated with two caryatids** was dismantled after 1945. Photo, 1940.

The POMPEIAN GALLERY has fresco painting echoing the Rafael Loggia ornamentation in the Vatican. This space was lit by five lantern-shaped chandeliers and was used as a restful retreat. Four landscape paintings in the antique fashion are set into a wall opposite the windows. Four arches divide the ceiling into separate miniature domes which are richly painted with mythical half-figures, animals, and birds of all earthly kinds. The ornamentation is exquisitely elegant and abundant in detail. Here Stakenschneider surpassed himself in his delicate contours and skilful application of colour which displayed all variety of hues and tones of white.

103 **The Pompeian Gallery** is famous for its fresco paintings echoing the Rafael Loggia ornamentation in the Vatican. Photo, late 19C.

104 **Detail of one of the colourful mural paintings.** Antique style fresco on a mythological scene.

105, 106 **Painted arches and ceiling** of the Pompeian Gallery display all variety of contours, hues and tones.

107 **Detail** of the painted ceiling of the Library. Medallions are set in the lunettes, portraying celebrated thinkers, scholars and poets throughout the ages.

Five windows provide an abundance of light in the LIBRARY, which is isolated from any noise and is wonderfully quiet. It is devoid of bright colours, preference being given to softer, pale tones. The Library contained over 50 thousand volumes. Above the low bookcases nine stylized medallions were set into the walls, portraying distinguished thinkers, poets and scholars throughout the ages: Petrarch, Shakespeare, Milton, Dante, Descartes, Galilei, Ariosto, Tasso and Calderon. The choice is believed to have been agreed with the Duke of Leuchtenberg, who was famous for his broad outlook on life and keen scientific interests. Wide desks displayed prints. "It is a treasury of science and art... in a way, a scholarly institution with its own law and order",[19] wrote N.Kukolnick, emphasizing the unusual location of the Library, not in a private area near the master's study, but almost accessible to other people as well, more about which we will discuss later.

108 **Detail** of one of the medallions portraying Dante.

109 **Library.** Photo, late 19C.

110 **The Oval family Dining-Room.**
Photo, late 19C.

The Library had a doorway into the oval FAMILY DINING-ROOM used for daily meals and dinners with friends. The room is an attractive beige colour. The focal point is a narrow multifigure stucco frieze in NeoGreek style featuring 35 scenes from the life of Alexander the Great of Macedonia. The frieze is believed to have been designed according to the drawings of the Danish sculptor Bertel Thorwaldsen, who was much admired by the Leuchtenbergs. The Ionic columns here are faced in scagliola and emphasize the chaste Classic design of the room.

111 **The Oval Dining-Room** was intended for family meals and small receptions of close friends. Classical decor is most simple.

The compact layout of the gala rooms along the palace axis, interconnected by numerous doors, meant that the interior could be turned into a single entity, comfortable and spacious enough to accomodate many guests who had an opportunity to enjoy the indoor garden freshness during the winter ball season.

113 **Carrara marble fireplace** in the Oval Dining-Room.

112 **The Oval Dining-Room** has a narrow multifigure sculptured frieze with 35 scenes in relief depicting 'Return of Alexander of Macedonia' executed from the designs by the Danish sculptor B.Thorwaldsen.

To the west of the Square Room is the OVAL PARLOUR of the Grand Duchess where the richly painted coffered ceiling, enhanced with gold, draws most attention. The alabaster caryatids are also worthy of note as are the wonderful white marble fireplace and fine parquet floor with a tinted wooden frieze. Comfortable furniture for this room was commissioned from the fashionable cabinetmakers A.Tur and H.Gambs, and the quiet, relaxing atmosphere encouraged friendly talks. Here Maria liked to sit surrounded by her friends, mostly writers and artists whom she always patronized. Ordinary guests were not admitted to this room.

114 **Fireplace of the Oval Parlour** has a lovely ornation in relief flanking the heater, featuring a girl in long attire holding flowers, and blossoming bushes in the frieze.

115 **The Oval Parlour of Maria Nikolayevna.** Detail of the painted ceiling in its central part.

116 **The semi-circular flanks of the ceiling in the Oval Parlour** are divided into four sectors of terracotta background. Each sector reveals a female mask in a medallion framed by cherubs and swans.

Private rooms are situated in the right wing of the building. The rooms facing St. Isaac's Square were used by Maximilian, and included a billiard room, a sitting room and a study. The picture collection makes for a special story.

The SITTING ROOM featured a heavily moulded ceiling with painting and details picked out in gold; two inlaid rosewood doors made in the same manner as the doors of the Gala Reception Room, and a fireplace in grey marble decorated with stone-like shells.

A wonderful collection of arms and antique weapons was on show, among which several items had once belonged to Eugène de Beauharnais and Emperor Napoléon I. The wallcases contained a marvellous mineral collection. Eventually it was transferred to the Mineral Cabinet of the Academy of Sciences in Munich. The furniture was an example of simple but exquisite taste. Following on from these rooms were the Turkish Room, a bathroom and the servants' quarters.

Maria's private rooms display an array of historic styles.

The Florentine Renaissance style prevails in her RECEPTION ROOM. It is almost devoid of natural daylight, but seems very light because of the soft

117 **Reception Room of the Grand Duchess** evinces Florentine Renaissance style. This tiny room is almost devoid of natural light, but seems bright because of the soft tones of the scagliola walls and the abundant white moulding. The focus is on the unusual three quarter length columns adorned with flower garlands and tiny medallions.

tones of the scagliola walls and the abundant delicate white mouldings. Most attractive are the unusual three quarter length paired columns, which are fluted at the base and have gilded moulded arabesques, and bird designs and floral garlands set in relief.

119 **Reception Room.**
Photo, late 19C.

118 **Detail of one of the columns**
in Reception Room of the Grand Duchess.

Maria's STUDY is also decorated in Florentine Renaissance style. Its four tetrahedral pillars and pilasters feature delicately moulded Grotesque ornamentation highlighted in gold, and miniature medallions. Similar, but larger elegant medallions which display the stylized portraits of philosophers and warriors are set into a frieze. The pillars divide the room into two unequal parts, which were once separated by

120 **Maria's Study** is decorated in Florentine Renaissance style. Rich ornate pillars divide the room into two unequal parts.

121 The smaller part of the Study has a white marble fireplace.

122 **Caissoned ceilings** are a particular success of Stakenschneider.

a heavy velvet curtain. The caissoned ceiling has two main hexahedral coffers of different shape and size and covered with damask. Drollinger was responsible for the painting en grisaille, featuring little children with a dog and a lamb and other ornamentation, each with its own inimitable pattern so that every ceiling in the palace is different.

123 **Tetrahedral columns** abound in delicate mouldings highlighted with gold.

124 **Maria's Study** has a mosaic fireplace of detailed pattern in its frieze and side pilasters featuring a lion, an eagle feeding two eaglets, a snake, a crane and a peacock, and Medusa's head and antique masks.

Two fireplaces furnish the room, one of them beautifully decorated with a detailed mosaic. The playwright Kukolnick mentioned rich furniture, in particular the antique cabinets, as well as pictures by Ivan Aivazovsky, Timothy Neff, Tyronov, etc.

125 **Detailed frieze** motif of the mosaic fireplace in the Study.

127 **A lovely ormolu chandelier** is hanging from the magnificently caissoned ceiling in the smaller part of the Study.

126 **The white marble fireplace** in the Study has a beautifully carved frieze featuring Venus at the Forge of Vulcan.

128 **Maria's Study.** The caissoned ceiling boasts rich ornamentation and painted scenes executed by Drollinger.

129 E.STÖCKLER, ***Bedchamber of the Grand Duchess,*** 1850—60. State Russian Museum, St. Petersburg. Publication of A.V.Maximova. Formerly this painting was catalogued as "an unknown interior by an unknown artist".

The BEDROOM is entirely different: the walls are painted in rich dark olive and brownish tones. The alcove ceiling has a fresco of the 'Sleeping Venus' reminiscent of the eternally young and captivating goddess by Giorgione. The ceiling and frieze are embellished with fantastic pictures of nymphs and the Graces, companions of Venus, and scenes of twilight and dawn. The letters of Maria's name formed into the same gilded moulded motif as in the vestibule on the ground floor can be seen in an apex of the extensively decorated scagliola arch over the bed alcove. The same motif can also be found in smaller letters atop the mantlepiece of the gorgeous fireplace of black marble veined with orange, and in very tiny letters on the carved gilded curtain rails.

130, 131 **Maria's Bedroom** in Renaissance style. The frieze features acanthus fronds, mythical characters and masks. The ceiling is embellished with small fresco scenes of twilight and dawn, depicting nymphs and Graces, the companions of Venus. The scagliola arch over the bed alcove is rich in detailed moulding and delicate gilding.

132 **Bedroom.** A gorgeous fireplace of black marble veined with orange. The heater is faced in white tiles. Elaborate stucco mantlepiece has niches and a bas-relief depicting frolicking cherubs.

133 **The name** of the mistress of the palace is atop the mantlepiece.

134 **A stucco gilded motif** spelling out Maria's name is topped with a crown and is shown at an apex of the arch.

135 **The same moulded motif** in very tiny letters is set in the carved gilded curtain rails of the Bedroom.

136 **The bed alcove arch.** The alcove ceiling with a fresco of the 'Sleeping Venus' evokes Giorgione's goddess.

137 **Octagonal Bathroom** in NeoClassical style. Four different stucco caryatids in long tunics, each repeated twice, support the architrave.

The BATHROOM in Pompeian style has a cupola painted with scenes of 'The Toilette of Venus', restrained white scagliola walls and eight caryatids, in the form of antique handmaidens, therefore, it conjures up the association of a Roman patrician bath. The 'Toilette of Venus' is a favourite subject with poets and artists: cherubs (or the Graces) assist the goddess as she bathes, put a golden wreath on her perfumed hair, and help her with the magic girdle in which all the sorcery of love is held.

138 **White Carrara marble fireplace** in the Bathroom. The side pilasters feature torches in acanthus frond surrounds in relief, the frieze above the heater reveals a credence in acanthus leaf ornamentation.

Each of the eight ceiling paintings feature a different scene. The octagoal bathroom is adorned with eight marble pillars, the upper halves of which are designed in the shape of a caryatid each crowned by an Ionic capitel resembling an elaborate hairstyle. There are four different figures, each repeated twice: one holds a jewellery box, another a looking glass, another a bowl and the last one attends to the magic girdle.

139 **The 'Toilette of Venus'** is painted on the ceiling of the Bathroom. Gesso frames divide octagonal ceiling space into eight sectors with eight pictures featuring cherubs assisting Venus as she bathes.

The Rococo BOUDOIR (in Louis XV style) resembles a wedding candy box. Kukolnick wrote: "Once in the boudoir à la Pompadour one no longer feels like arguing: it makes one feel so fine, so merry, so grand. The focal point is hard to choose, all around there are mirrors; there is most elaborate gilded woodcarving; there is damask of silky splendour; and several pictures à la Watteau. It is a dazzling mixture of elegant bric-a-brac in its infinite multitude".[20] The fireplace here is particularly exquisite: an ordinary copper heater was set into a container fashioned in porcelain, richly painted and highlighted in gold. It was made in the 1840s at the Imperial porcelain works.

140 **The Rococo Boudoir**
(à la Pompadour).
Photo, c.1940.

141, 142 **Ornamentation details** after Stakenschneider drawings.

The semicircular shape of the Corner STUDY prompted the pattern of the moulded and delicately painted ceiling. In one of the corners is an attractive fireplace in colourful marble, with a central terracotta panel carved after a mythological tale. The walls originally boasted pictures by Antonio Correggio, Guido Reni, and Carlo Dolci among other Western masters. This room was connected to the Duke's suite by a hearing tube. A French door served as the entrance from the broad balcony complemented by the garden ramp. When fully furnished Grand Duchess Maria's rooms, lavishly and gracefully decorated with damask and silk upholstery, with mirrors and furniture of the highest craftsmanship, must have been simply stunning, so exquisite was every item , so completely complementary to each interior.

Well-known artists and craftsmen interpreted Stakenschneider's sketches to produce an excellent interior finish; the same team also implemented his later designs. The masters Yaishnikov, Kosolapov and Dylev executed plasterworks. Memoirs note the particular fondness with which

143 **Fireplace** of white, grey and red marble in the Corner Study. A mosaic panel with a colourful marble border in white marble surround. The central panel features a reclining female with a looking glass (Venus?) assisted by two cherubs.

144 **Small Corner Study** of the Grand Duchess with a French window onto the broad balcony and the garden ramp.

145 **Small Corner Study.** Its semicircular shape required a special pattern of the exquisitely painted and moulded ceiling. Under the Soviets, Maria's name in stucco relief disappeared from the ceiling.

146 **Drawing of the Corner Study ceiling** by Stakenschneider.

the architect used to sketch designs for minutely detailed items of bronze, porcelain and furniture. The leading cabinetmakers of St. Petersburg, such as Heinrich Gambs, Andrey Tur and Vasili Bobkov made sets of furniture from those drawings. Highly valued was furniture incorporating some novelty of the period: springs in the seat, quilted upholstery, tables and armchairs on rollers.

Hereditary parquet makers from the Tarassov family executed fine floors using Stakenschneider's sketches. The local carpenters also made individual pieces of furniture from his designs such as doors in costly inlay, and remodelled a few unfashionable doors which were transferred to the palace from the Engineers' Castle.[21] Apart from that, they fashioned the doors after the Munich originals, and the perfect craftsmanship made it hard to tell which door had been brought from Germany and which had been made by the skilful Russian masters.

147 **The Church Staircase** was painted in Byzantine style after a design by the artist Prince G.G.Gagarin. It was partly restored in the 1980s.

148 **Our Lady of Korsun** above the entrance to the Oratory. Painted in imitation of a mosaic designed by G.G.Gagarin.

The family CHURCH of St.Nicholas the Miracle-Worker, in Byzantine style in the attic storey, right above the Gala Reception room, originally received light through five skylights in the ceiling. "This minute place is astonishing in its sumptuousness, gracefulness and splendour",[22] the Petersburg Leaflet (Listok) assured its readers in 1885. The walls and the pinewood iconostasis were previously plain white. The carvings and central gate (the so-called Holy Gate) of the iconostasis were richly gilded. The altar icons and the iconostasis were originally painted by Academician C. Duzzi. Eventually Maria wanted the walls and ceiling to be decorated in fresco. In 1856—60, the biblical scenes were designed by the family friend and artist Prince Grigory Gagarin, the then Vice-President of the Academy of Arts. He was also commissioned to rebuild the altar part of the Church. The choice of subjects by Maria was not accidental: they all reveal the display of Jesus' grace to women — 'Healing by Touch', 'The Healing of the Widow's Son at Nain', 'Jesus and an Adulteress', 'Jesus, Martha and Maria' and 'The Assumption' among others.

150 **The family Church** of St.Nicholas the Miracle-Worker. The central painting on the southern wall. Biblical scenes were designed by Prince Gagarin, the then Vice-President of the Academy of Arts, as a special commission by Grand Duchess Maria.

149 **'Jesus and a Samaritan woman'** has more or less survived as the most authentic painting by Gagarin. Before 1940, the Church was used as a lecture hall, after World War II, as a cinema. Therefore, nearly 85% of the original painting was lost.

151 **The family Church** of St.Nicholas in Byzantine style is being restored. Painted arches, the ceiling and pillars have been restored after the fragments of the original ornamentation made in 1856—60.

The murals were fashioned after Gagarin's drawings by the artist M.Troshchinsky in a special mastic of his own make. His resinous 'paint' was made to a special recipe in specific proportions; it dried out in a few minutes, had no offensive odour, did not go off and was damp-proof. "The panicadilo of the church is most exquisite", a contemporary remembered, "It consists of a cross-shaped candlestick which has icon-lamp mats instead of candles, creating a wonderfully conducive spiritual atmosphere".[23]

Maria Nikolayevna ordered special festive vestments for the priest and the deacon; the vestry by the altar was dressed in blue velvet with a silver pattern; for everyday wear vestments of green cloth were commissioned with the pattern of a cross in silver. The priest's robes were made of crimson velvet. There was also a third set of robes for Holy Week. The stairs to the Church were decorated by the best professors of the Academy of Arts in Byzantine style.

152 **The family Church** of St.Nicholas the Miracle-Worker. Photo, c.1880s.

153 **Detail** of one of the paintings. 'Jesus and an Adultress'. The technique is similar to encaustic.

An ORATORY which originally adjoined the Church did not have a complete iconostasis, but consisted only of its major section, the Holy Gate. The icons of the Holy Gate were based on the mosaic icons at St. Sophia in Kiev: the Annunciation, the Evangelists, the Divine Teachers, and the Deacons. Among the best icons were The Trinity in the old Greek manner, The Vladimir Mother of God, and an oakwood icon-case with local saints among others. Most of the icons were family relics, and a few of them were wedding gifts, apart from the icon with which Maria's marriage was blessed by her parents.

Contemporary reports also record the beauty of the Catholic church built on the ground floor for the Duke of Leuchtenberg. A particularly remarkable feature there was a stained glass panel, depicting the Mother of God and two saints — Maximilian and Eugène. The panel was made at the Royal factory in Munich in 1842.

154 **An icon** in an oak icon-case from the Oratory. 1859. From a design by the architect A.M.Gornostayev.

On the ground floor near the ramp were the south-facing nurseries and the rooms of the English governesses. Between the Entrance Hall and the Winter Garden, in the very centre of the ground floor, there was a huge RECREATION HALL which had 11 doors. It was heated by two marble fireplaces. When the boys were small, the hall was used for incessant physical training under the supervision of their tutors. Later the adult young Dukes of Leuchtenberg played the then fashionable lawn-tennis there with their Romanov relatives.

Recreation halls in the homes of aristocrats were a rarity at that time. Stakenschneider designed another one at the Grand Duke Nicholas' Palace on Annunciation (Blagoveshchensky) Square.

Almost 60 pleasantly furnished rooms on the upper floor were used as bedrooms and parlours for the numerous courtiers of Maria and Max. The courtiers' quarters also extended to two further wings facing onto the streets and the yard.

In all, Stakenschneider not only met the functional requirements of his clients, but also demonstrated his great mastery, employed unique engineering techniques and architectural solutions, and managed to show sensitivity to changing styles and trends. Moreover, he created a splendid emotional artistic atmosphere in the interior which pleased the young mistress. The Tsar, who was rather an authority on architecture and considered himself an art expert, oversaw the construction with particular care. The Duke of Leuchtenberg also shared this supervisory role. The erudition and the sense of beauty which distinguished the young owners of the palace helped to bring the project to perfection. But it was Stakenschneider, with his agreeable, tactful and patient character, able to withstand the monarch's whims, who proved his creative ingenuity with this project.

155 Ch.ROBERTSON, ***Portrait of Grand Duchess Maria Nikolayevna, wife of Duke of Leuchtenberg, with their children Maria, Eugenia, Nicholas and Evguen,*** 1849. State Russian Museum, St. Petersburg. Before requisition in 1920s, the portrait belonged to George Maximilianovich Duke of Leuchtenberg.

156 *Maximilian and Maria Nikolayevna,* lith. par H.Schmid, c. 1840.

The Duke received many visitors at the Maryinsky Palace all reported to him by his aide Prince Bagratyon. Apart from his military service, Maximilian had other duties and interests. He studied galvanoplastics and electrochemical metallurgy, and had a laboratory, initially, at the Winter Palace and then at the Guards' Headquarters. Maximilian's research made great headway in galvanoplastics, and presumably the eminent Krupp could have gone bankrupt without Maximilian's scientific achievements. In 1847, the Duke of Leuchtenberg was working on the production and raffination of copper by electrolysis, and the separation of gold and silver. Much later the same method was employed in North America.

157 **Detailed lithograph** of Maximilian and Maria.

In the outskirts of Petersburg, beyond the Obvodny (Bypass) Canal near the Baltic railway station, Max built a plant. The street where it was located retained the name of Leuchtenberg Street until 1917. The plant produced not only fine quality ormolu artworks by electrolysis, but also the first locomotives in Russia. Those locomotives were very successful and served the railroad to Tsarskoye Selo and Warsaw. The galvanoplastic shops of the plant were commissioned to produce nearly all the statues for the arches and the cupola drum inside St. Isaac's which was then under construction. Even after the Duke died, correspondence yet went on, as the building committee in charge of the Cathedral of Christ the Redeemer in Moscow (arch. C.Ton) ordered a supply of copper gilded chains from the works for the domes of the Moscow church (1855).

Maximilian, who by then had become an honorary member of the Academy of Sciences, was also very keen on mining and mineralogy, and he studied mining technology. In 1844 the Tsar appointed him Head of the Mining Engineering department. Upon his death, a note was found in his papers which read: "I was always happy to act as Head of the Institute of Mining Engineers, this work brought me consolation and contentment".[24] As requested in his will, the Duke's widow handed his uniform and sword over to the Institute of Mining Engineers for permanent storage.

In 1843, after the death of Alexei Olenin, the then President of the Academy of Arts, and an eminent archaeologist and Director of the Imperial Public Library, a decision was taken to entrust the Art Academy leadership entirely to members of the Imperial family. The Sovereign appointed his son-in-law President of the Art Academy. The Vice-President Count Feodor Tolstoy, famous sculptor and medal-maker, was in charge of the day to day running of the Academy, for the Duke's military duties made him leave Petersburg rather often. The monarch's choice was not accidental: Max painted in oil and drew fairly well, and he inherited the famous Munich picture gallery. The collection had been gathered by his father Eugène de Beauharnais and much augmented in the days when the latter had been created HIH Prince français, Arch Chancellor of the Empire, Prince of Venice, installed as Viceroy of the Kingdom of Italy, and Hereditary Grand Duke of Frankfurt. The collection was celebrated for its excellent works by the Italian masters Giovanni Bellini, Agnolo Bronzino, Raphael Sanzio, Bernardino Luini, Lorenzo Lotto, the Dutch masters Jan Steen, Gabriel Metsu, the Dutch marine painter Ludolf Backhuysen, who had been a teacher of Peter the Great, the Flemish painters Hans Memling and Anthony van Dyck and the Spanish painters Diego Velazquez and Bartolome Murillo. Most of the paintings left Munich for St. Petersburg where they decorated the Duke's apartments at the Maryinsky. By right of primogeniture the gallery passed to the eldest son Duke Nicholas Maximilianovich.

158 **One of a pair of ormolu candelabra** produced at the Duke's works. Palace Museum, Gatchina.

179

In 1868, the publisher M.Wulf in St. Petersburg printed graphic copies of the best 43 paintings of the collection thus enabling everybody to enjoy that wealth. Below we tell how the collection was divided between the heirs. A small part of it was later nationalized and taken to the Hermitage in Leningrad and the Moscow galleries. Max also became a benevolent friend of eminent Russian artists, and he bought first class paintings from them, collecting the works of Carl Briullov, Timothy Neff and Ivan Aivazovsky among others.

In the science world the Duke had several admirers who appreciated his broad knowledge of natural sciences. Academician B.S.Jacobi held his talent in high esteem and used to call him 'a flown-in eagle'. Indeed, a real scholar had not appeared in the Imperial family until Maximilian. The time had not yet come for such erudites in science as the historian Nicholas Mikhailovich, the poet, playwright, musician and actor Constantine Constantinovich (K.R.), and the neumismatist and art researcher George Mikhailovich, to emerge among grand dukes. Anyway, Maria always proudly mentioned to her new friends that her husband was a scholar. In the Urals, local mine explorers and industrialists also boasted that, for the first time, the mining business was in the hands of a competent member of the Tsar's family.

A country estate in the Tambov province, which Max had bought after selling his Italian lands to the papal government, was regarded as a model farm. (Incidentally, a villa on the Tambov estate was also built by Stakenschneider.) The ward committee established for Maria's children after Max died recorded the farm as being consistently profitable.

In 1846, a charitable society 'Visiting the Poor' was established in Petersburg with the Duke of Leuchtenberg as its patron. The main concern of the Society was the spreading poverty in the capital, and the urgent need to separate the desperately poor from professional beggars. Its members managed to set up various institutions, family flats with workshops, the sale of produce brought in by poor people, paid for immediately in cash, and prison inspection among others. The only surviving institution was the Maximilianovski Hospital for the poor (1850) in the former Maximilianovski Lane which was a prototype of the contemporary outpatient clinics. That medical institution happened to be the first free clinic for visiting poor patients in Europe. Grand Duchess Helena Pavlovna later became its benefactress (1855—73), and was replaced by her daughter Catherine (up to 1894). The last benefactress until 1917 was Max's daughter Eugenia who married Alexander Prince of Oldenburg. Ironically the original free clinic for the poor became the first and, for dozens of years, the only medical institution in Leningrad to charge for treatment under the Bolsheviks, retaining its name Maximilianovski until the present day.

Count V.Sollogub related how deeply involved Maximilian was in his committee work, and how much he enjoyed the informal efficient atmosphere of their meetings and debates until the early hours of the morning. Occasionally Max was informed that the Grand Duchess had arrived to remind him that it was high time to go back home.

His private life was a source of much gossip at Court. A.Tiutcheva reputed him as "a handsome fellow, a gambler and a debauchee..."[25], a sort of profligate, and the Duke made no secret of his love affairs. Presumably the marriage, once formed on love, turned later into a mere formality. It's worth remembering that the courtship of beautiful ladies was the order of the day and regarded almost as a necessity for genuine aristocrats. However, the Duke's busy way of life and earnest interests make us doubt the sincerity and justice of Tiutcheva's statement. Most of his contemporaries considered Max to be a wonderful character, a genuine Frenchman with excellent manners, kind disposition and appeal, with a great sense of humour and of everything noble and beautiful.

Some memoirs which concur with entries in Olga's diary testify that Max was not happy in Russia. Military duties became a burden, now and again "they made him feel a stranger, a foreigner. He was appointed Commander of a joint brigade of Lancer and Horse-grenadier Guards whose duty was to parade daily in front of the Tsar's windows at Peterhof. Uncle Michael insisted on the most rigid attention to the Prussian type drill which inevitably caused much despair and misfortune". Grand Duke Michael would burst out shouting, begging the Tsar not to interfere, and peace was only reinstated upon the arrival of the Heir Apparent. Olga sympathized greatly with her relative who happened to come to live "in the land of semicivilized customs, morals and manner... among people who speak and think differently, where the most severe climate continued to ruin his health".[26]

Duke Maximilian lived a short life. After catching a cold during a Urals works inspection journey, he never recovered. He tried to find a cure for his illness in Estonia and in other countries abroad. Gradually people got used to talks about his grave illness (TB). Maximilian Duke of Leuchtenberg died on 20 October, 1852, and was buried at St. John of Jerusalem Chapel on the Corps de Pages grounds, where he had once dreamed of the realm of happiness. Maria informed her sister-in-law Joséphine, the Queen of Sweden and Norway, that she had ordered a sarcophagus designed as "an altar of Max's favourite marble, as the one in St. Isaac's. It is green and reminiscent of an ancient image of death".[27] According to his will, Max's heart was transferred to Munich for burial at the family sepulchre. Maria wrote to her Bavarian relations: "Our Family mourns over our son, the army grieves their comrade, the middle class mourns over their

Madeira 1849.
C. Brulloff

dess. sur pierre par Smirnoff.

Lithogr. de l'Adm. princip. des ponts et des chauss. (Cte Pohl Dir.)

friend".[28] The children adored their father. The Emperor went into deep mourning and ordered the Court and nation into three months mourning, as though for the death of a grand duke.

When her husband was alive, Maria Nikolayevna was noted for her charitable deeds. In all, she remained an integral part of the Petersburg high life where vanity and the thirst for pleasure were overriding and prevailed over serious interests and moral obligations. She enjoyed looking beautiful and feeling men's admiration. And who can cast a stone at a woman of such high breeding allowed to feast as she did at this table of life? Many loved her gay manner and quick wit. Several found her wayward, cynical, vulgar. Her mother-in-law was appalled when she saw Maria smoking, especially as she tried to introduce the bad habit to Linda, Max's younger sister, so that both of them smelled terribly of tobacco. Other people confirmed Tiutcheva's words that she was "an extremely capable and gifted creature who combined astonishing beauty and keen wit, an affable character and a wonderful heart, but that she lacked lofty ideals, spiritual and intellectual zeals".[29]

Curious enough that Maria Nikolayevna was never addressed as the Duchess of Leuchtenberg after one memorable outburst of rage by Nicholas I at a ball. The Emperor was talking to the Austrian ambassador Ficquelmont when Maria's new young gentleman in attendance approached, interrupted the Tsar, and loudly related to Count Ficquelmont that the Duchess of Leuchtenberg requested the honour of dancing the first polonaise with Mr. Ambassador. The Emperor was furious. After calling the boy a fool, he impressed upon the spectators that his daughter was first and foremost Her Imperial Highness Grand Duchess, and not Duchess of Leuchtenberg, and that she extended the honour by inviting anyone to dance to her. The young man was fired, the head man in attendance was severely rebuked for choosing such a stupid person without manners for the job. Indeed, the Duchess Mother and other relations were said to suffer in the belief that their beloved Max was not a real master in his home, and were grieved that the Maryinsky did not turn into the Palais de Leuchtenberg.

It has to be said that the Grand Duchess was also not renowned for her fidelity. It was not by accident that she was reproached for being morally weak and for her many love affairs. There is a well-known episode as told by Count Peter A. Shuvalov, Chief of 3rd Section of Gendarmerie in the reign of Alexander II, to A. A. Polovtsov, the Imperial Secretary, which rather defines this attitude to marriage.

Once, at a fancy dress ball at the Karamzins, Maria approached Shuvalov and persuaded him to take her to another fancy dress ball at the Assembly of Noblemen. When they arrived there, Shuvalov handed the Grand Duchess' sable coat to the cloak attendant in the hallway, but kept the

159 K.P.BRIULLOV, *Portrait of Maximilian Duke of Leuchtenberg,* 1849. Private collection, Brussels.

costly sable boots in his uniform pocket. Some time later he saw how the Grand Duchess took Karamzin[30] by the hand, the latter presumably having left his own ball by prior mutual agreement. Feeling lonely and bored Shuvalov went out to inquire about Maria's fur coat. But great was his amazement on learning that the Grand Duchess had departed leaving her boots in Shuvalov's pocket! The enraged Shuvalov returned to the hall where "he saw the Duke of Leuchtenberg strolling with a courtesan. He gave the boots to the Duke and explained how he had got them". Maximilian exploded and wanted to challenge Shuvalov to a duel, but matters were quietly settled.[31] Years after, Maria Nikolayevna cried bitterly at Karamzin's death defending Sebastopol, and with all her heart tried to console his widow and sisters.

The liaison with Count Grigory Alexandrovich Stroganov (1823—78) began when her husband was still alive (it was affirmed that her son George Maximilianovich, born in 1852, and Stroganov were like two peas in a pod). In 1854, Grand Duchess Maria married Stroganov morganatically. "Emperor Nicholas would never agree to a marriage of his daughter to any one of his subjects", wrote Tiutcheva. She assured her readers: if the Tsar knew how matters really were, he would probably send Stroganov to the Caucasus, where war was being waged, and force his daughter into a convent. Hence, the utmost secrecy of their wedding, held in the private church of Countess Potyomkina. Tsesarevich Alexander and his spouse Maria discreetly witnessed the event. Nicholas I died in February 1855 in ignorance of the wedding. On learning the news, the Dowager Empress Alexandra called that marriage the most bitter grief after the death of the Emperor, "the grief of being cheated by her own children".[32]

Such a shocking event in the Imperial family was almost unprecedented except for the morganatic marriage in 1820 of Tsesarevich Constantine Pavlovich and the young Countess Joanna Grudzinska of Poland. But the special State Manifesto of Alexander I announced the marriage, and also stated that their issue had no rights to the throne. This made Constantine later renounce his rights to the throne officially. But there followed no official announcement of Maria's marriage, although its official date was noted as 16 November 1856. Was it erratic love? Boundless courage in the hope that she would find forgiveness from her loving parents? Who can tell? The event only confirms how resolute and unpredictable the Maryinsky mistress was. According to Dmitri Miliutin, a fieldmarshal-general and military historian of Russia, high society looked upon Maria's romance and marriage as the rebellion of a passionate individual protesting against the senseless rigid formality at Court and in the Tsar's Family.

Count Grigory Stroganov neither became an integral part of the House of Romanov, nor did high society favour him. He was soon created

160 T.A.NEFF, *Portrait of Grand Duchess Maria Nikolayevna, President of Art Academy,* St. Petersburg. 1850—60. The portrait was probably commissioned to decorate the Meeting Hall of the Council where all the portraits of the Academy Presidents, from that of Ivan Shuvalov to Maria Pavlovna, Sr., were displayed.

lieutenant-general and marshall of his spouse's court. He developed an interest in archaeology and, like a real Stroganov, had a passion for minerals, for which he was appointed chaperone to accompany the Crown Prince Nicholas when the latter travelled throughout Russia. The story is that he was very handsome when younger, a nice natural fellow without any swaggering, a real carouser who never changed until he died.

More and more often, Maria and Stroganov would go abroad where they stayed for long periods. From 1862 onwards, they frequented the villa Quarto near Florence which she bought from A.Demidov, Prince of San Donato (once the villa belonged to Napoléon's brother, King of Westphalia), and had the villa refurbished. Her life in Italy and France offered the possibility to buy fine paintings, as she used to turn her ear to the words of experts and special advisors. Baron N.N. Wrangel wrote about the wholesale purchase of the gallery of the Irish Count Cotherell, and later traced how it was divided up among Maria's heirs.

The habit of squandering money when her father was alive much embarrassed Maria during the reign of Emperor Alexander II. In 1867, when Shuvalov accompanied the monarch on his visit of Paris, the Grand Duchess begged Shuvalov to get a few thousand francs out of the Tsar. She assured him that she had no money to pay the hotel bill. The Tsar refused point-blank and added that his sister had long been abusing that source.

The way of life of Maria and Max never made the Maryinsky one of the celebrated salons such as the legendary salons of the Michael and Marble Palaces, with their enchanting balls, musical and theatrical performances, and concerts in which the hosts performed. Maria's first short and confused marriage did not establish many traditions. The family lived together at this palace for less than eight years when Maximilian was alive, and the Duke remained gravely ill for the last period. Above all, within 13 years of her first marriage Maria gave birth to 7 children. Their first daughter Alexandra (1840—43) died early and was buried at SS. Peter & Paul's. An infant son Nicholas was of poor health and underwent four operations in all, being constantly treated by the best orthopaedic specialists in Europe. In 1853, he stayed at an orthopaedic clinic in Germany. "That treatment resulted in the total failure of a bad leg, which became shorter and a chest pain started due to a daily ten hour machine stretch",[33] wrote Duke Nicholas. The eminent Russian surgeon Nicholas Pirogov rescued him, stating at a doctors' conference, organized by Maria in despair at the failure of her son's general health: "If he were my own son, I'd quit all machines and use gymnastics alone". With these words and a bow he withdrew. Luckily, they did so. There were also problems with the other children.

There were however many lavish parties and fancy dress balls, charity bazaars, and Christmas parties for children held at the Maryinsky.

161 T.A.NEFF, ***Detail of Maria Nikolayevna's portrait.*** The President's badge encrusted with diamonds is pinned on her shoulder.

A son Altesse Impériale

MADAME LA GRANDE DUCHESSE

Marie Nicolaewna

Duchesse de Leuchtenberg.

WIEGENLIED

pour le

PIANO

par

Adolphe Henselt.

Prix 45 kr. A: de C.

Proprieté des Editeurs. Enregistre dans l'Archive de l Union

VIENNE

chez Pietro Mechetti qm Carlo

Marchand de Musique et de beaux Arts de la Cour J. et Re

PARIS chez M. Schlesinger

St PETERSBOURG a l'Odéon, Dépot de Musique

162 Well known composers dedicated their music to Grand Duchess Maria. A *Lullaby* was presented by Adolf Henselt, a pianist and composer probably to mark the birth of one of Maria's children.

Amateur performances were staged in the Rotunda and Square Room (Count Sollogub wrote a comedy 'The Civil Officer' for the court stage). Most often they enjoyed 'charades en action', and gladly hosted high-life celebrities, and famous people in the sciences, art and literature. Among their guests were the architect Stakenschneider, the poet Zhukovsky, the publisher and Petersburg University rector Pletnev who had formerly taught Russian language and literature to the Tsesarevich and Maria in their teens (while visiting Paris, Maria went to see the old sick teacher), the writer and social figure Prince Odoyevsky, and the poet and critic Prince Viazemsky. Private correspondence between Zhukovsky and his friends confirms Maria's permanent interest in literature. Curious is the fact that the Grand Duchess invited writer Nicholas Gogol to come to see her during her stay in Rome. Gogol always avoided high society, but as an exception, he did put on a black tail-coat, which he had had to borrow.

In the palace Concert Hall, both professional singers and musicians and amateur talented aristocrats performed, such as the violinist and composer Lvov, and the two brothers Wielgorsky, the noted musicians and patrons of liberal arts. Matthew Wielgorsky, a wonderful cellist, was appointed Marshall of Maria's court and served her, from her wedding day until his death in 1856. Before he passed away, Count Matthew handed over his famous Stradivari cello which he used to call 'my wife' to the young cellist Davidov who thereafter often played at Maryinsky Palace in memory of his late friend.

Yet the Emperor was the most frequent guest. "Barely a day passed without a visit of us", his grandson Nicholas recollected.[34] That boy's birth on 23 July 1843 was a sheer Family joy as he was the first Tsar's grandson, and the Emperor was thrilled. That day the Tsar arrived from manoeuvres at Koporye town to the Sergievka villa for congratulations. Duke Nicholas treasured a small painting: Nicholas I sitting in a carriage pulled by four grey horses, wearing a white Horse Guards cap on the way back to Koporye.

Strict court etiquette was observed only at balls and official receptions, otherwise the Grand Duchess remained a cordial hostess, witty, humorous, affable, and an enlightened benefactress.

The palace abounded in valuable art works and family relics, from the Empress Joséphine's diamonds to the small velveted containers with the locks of hair belonging to Joséphine and Napoléon among other rarities and historic objects. The family archive contained a nearly unique portrait of Max's grandfather, Viscount Alexander Françios de Beauharnais, who acted as Chairman of the Constituent Assembly, and was guillotined in Paris in 1794. Alexander de Beauharnais' correspondence with the people's deputies and the outstanding people of the day was inherited by George Nikolayevich Duke of Leuchtenberg. Most notable was the arms collection originally belonging to Napoléon and Eugène de Beauharnais.

The mistress of the palace added to her picture collection with great care and intelligence. The rooms were hung with the paintings of the Italian, German, French and Dutch masters: Bassano, Botticelli, Perugino, Tizian, Tiepolo, Greuze, Drouais, Mignard, Lucas Cranach, Jr., Moreelse, Rembrandt, R.Hubert, Roslin, etc. After Grand Duchess Maria's death the collection was divided among her children from both her marriages.

After Duke Maximilian died, Maria's way of life drastically changed. There emerged new obligations and responsibility for the upbringing of her children. The order to the Senate of 3 November 1852 stated that HIH Grand Duchess Maria Nikolayevna was appointed President of the Art Academy. She stayed in office for 24 years. Upon her death she was succeeded by her nephew Grand Duke Vladimir Alexandrovich, and after the latter died in 1909 the post passed to his wife Grand Duchess Maria Pavlovna, Sr., who happened to be the final Romanov President of the Art Academy.

As an enlightened fan of the sciences and the arts, and a lady of all-round education, Maria showed keen interest in the future of national art. During her presidency the new Academy Rules were adopted (1859), lectures on old Russian art and liberal arts history were included, and a specific class on icon painting in the strict Byzantine style was introduced. The Academy Library and museums became accessible to the general public, and for the first time reader numbers increased to 2,500. The Academy building was also renovated. New areas were found for a museum of sculpture, and an architectural class among others. Measures were taken to accelerate the development of realistic and national trends in fine arts, which eventually helped the Itinerants to emerge.

Maria's presidency was also marked with the inauguration of a monument to Emperor Nicholas I which took place on 25 June 1859. The Grand Duchess herself supervised progress on the monument and frequented the foundry workshop of the sculptor Clodt at the Art Academy. The choice of the monument site was not surprising — the square in front of the Maryinsky Palace.

It took three years for the equestrian statue to be completed. Spectators relaxed when the huge statue on a wooden platform which had been mounting the Nikolayev Bridge on rollers finally crossed it. The platform was pulled by 60 workmen with two ropes fixed to the base of the statue. The bronze equestrian statue of Nicholas I was mounted onto a magnificent plinth of dark raspberry porphiry embellished with four bas-reliefs (sculp. N.Ramazanov), military accoutrements and four figures (sculp. R.Saleman). The seated female statues symbolizing Justice, Power, Wisdom and Faith bear some resemblance to Nicholas' wife and his three daughters.

163
V.I.TIMM,
Inauguration of the monument to Emperor Nicholas I in 1859.
'Art Leaflet by V.Timm', 1859.

164, 165 **View of St. Isaac's Square** and Statue of Nicholas I at present.

166 **Monument to Nicholas I** inaugurated in June 1859. One of the best equestrian statues in St. Petersburg (sc. P.Clodt, arch. A.Montferrand).

167 **A detail of the monument to Nicholas I.** Two forefigures represent Justice and Power (sc. R.Saleman).

The artist Timm's picture reveals the monument inauguration before the Imperial Family, the Court, and the diplomatic corps. The Court grenadiers in fur hats flank the area. Podiums are erected for spectators. A box for 7 persons would sell at 100 roubles, a chair at 25 roubles each, and it cost a rouble to stand on the far side. A rare rooftop glimpse of damsels' multicolour umbrellas was possible on this occasion. A window seat in a nearby house sold for 100 roubles, and a pair of theatre glasses cost 1 to 5 roubles.

A groundless rumour circulated that Maria Nikolayevna either disliked her palace or liked it less after the monument had been raised, because of the new window view onto the horse's tail.

Maria also became Chairperson of the Artists' Encouragement Society. The Society lacked a proper home and was destined to wander. At one time it based itself and its museum in the palace rooms of their august chairperson. A design school was arranged by the Society to qualify designers in textile manufacturing. Maria provided the school with art books from her own library, donated many valuable items to its museum, and she also insisted that the Sovereign grant a private house for the Society's activities.

Under her direct supervision there was also the Patriotic boarding school for girls of noble families, founded in 1827 and housed at No 3 on the Tenth Avenue of Vasilievsky Island. As famous and popular as the Smolny and Catherine schools in the mid-19th century, it was a privileged institution for the daughters of the hereditary gentry.

In bringing up her own children Maria Nikolayevna followed the system which Maximilian had introduced and which she remembered from her own childhood. "We were never pampered', wrote Duke Nicholas Maximilianovich. 'We rode in an open vehicle regardless of the weather, a closed carriage was allowed only when we had already caught a bad cold. Room temperature was around 10°—12° C, and bedrooms stayed particularly cold. We were only allowed to sleep in cots, in summer we used hay mattresses and very thin blankets".[35] The best teachers and professors were invited to tutor the eldest son in science especially as he inherited his father's aptitude. Their son Sergei was gifted in music and art, therefore the eminent art historian K.V.Liphart (from the Balts) was employed. Compulsory general fitness classes and military training which was a matter of importance at the time, were the order of the day. This typically strict upbringing was mandatory in the Romanov family, and the young Leuchtenbergs were also all expected to serve their country.

During the reign of Alexander II, Maria Nikolayevna who had aged unexpectedly, became much more involved in politics. It could have been because of the personal influence of the older sister on the august brother, or because of her high socio-political status and commitments. But whatever the reason, the political barometer recording the atmosphere at the

168 F.X.WINTERHALTER, ***Portrait of Grand Duchess Maria Nikolayevna,*** 1858. State Hermitage, St. Petersburg.

F.Winterhalter 1857.
Genève

Winter, the Michael and the Marble palaces, also pointed in the 1860s to the Maria Palace, where the views and attitudes remained moderately conservative. At one time, there was general unrest about her negative influence on the Sovereign in the matters of the liberation of serfs (according to Glinsky and the Miliutin brothers). Unlike her close relatives Grand Duke Constantine and Grand Duchess Helen, who became champions of the serf emancipation movement and who were the first to liberate their own serfs, Maria did not support the reformists. She was hostile to the outstanding reformist Nicholas Miliutin and, after once calling him Marate, in jest she proposed to act as Charlotte Corday. Witty Miliutin hitherto remarked tactfully that in no way would he agree to sit naked in a bath in front of Her Imperial Highness.

Pavel Valuev, the Minister of Interior, commented on the pleasant alterations in the private rooms of Empress Maria Alexandrovna at the Winter Palace, where the Golden Parlour and other apartments were refurbished into elegant salons due to new paintings, statues and furnishings. Alexander II not only trusted his sister's mind and taste, he also relied upon her moral support in the sensitive matter of the monarch's intimate life: notably his liaison with Princess Catherine Dolgoruky and the three children born by her out of wedlock. The Tsar's brothers Constantine and Nicholas, Sr., never reproached him for this as both of them had also developed permanent relationships with two other women and had had illegitimate children by them.

The Emperor's special affection towards Maria passed onto her children. Alexander II was evidently fond of his nephew Nicholas Duke of Leuchtenberg. A sole nephew among many others, this boy often accompanied the Tsar and his children during their travels throughout Russia. The eldest nephew who lost his father early, a son of the favourite sister, Duke Nicholas spent much time in the company of the Crown Prince Nicholas who was the same age, and of his cousins Alexander and Vladimir. The boy greatly impressed the monarch with his talent for science, and his keen mind, which distinguished him from his own offspring who were lazy and often received bad marks. At 16 years of age, once he had begun to master his university course, Duke Nicholas was granted a delay in military service and the privilege of leaving mandatory balls before the end, even prior to the Emperor's withdrawal.

In the 1860s, Grand Duchess Maria used to call herself 'an old woman' but her age never hampered her dynamism, eccentricity, unpredictable nature, openness and frankness. Prince Meshchersky observed that Maria's typically tsarish manner and behaviour never disappeared. It is in this light that he tells the story of Maria's Paris meeting with Emperor Napoléon III.

169
Ch.F.JALABERT,
Portrait of Grand Duchess Maria Nikolayevna, 1869.
State Hermitage,
St. Petersburg.

199

In 1864, Maria Nikolayevna stayed at a hotel in Paris where Emperor Napoléon III came to see her. With her royal bearing, and exhibiting the famous profile of her father she stood on the landing by her suite while the Emperor was ascending the stairs. She stretched out her hand, and he bent and kissed it. Then, a curious quid pro quo (lat. mess) took place by the doors.

As was customary in Paris, Napoléon wanted to enter Maria's room in a topcoat, with a walking stick in his hand. But Maria while standing in the doorway reminded him amiably but firmly: 'Sire, you are entering my salon'. The words were twice repeated before the Emperor stopped and looked around. 'Take His Majesty's coat away' Maria ordered in French. After such an official and dignified introduction she proceeded to friendly family discussions once in her salon.

170 **The endless funeral procession** stretching from the palace portico to the burial place at SS. Peter & Paul's, across the icebound Neva river. At its centre, Emperor Alexander II on horseback follows the funeral chariot.

171 **View in front of Maryinsky Palace and the catafalque** at the main entrance in February 1876, on Maria's burial day.

Maria Nikolayevna died on 9 February 1876 "after a long and grave disease", the State Manifesto read." A life abounding in light and shade came to an end. A life of so many colourful and meaningful chapters!" wrote Valuev in his diary.[36] At requiem, her body was carried solemnly from her private rooms into the Rotunda by the Sovereign and grand dukes. Her sons and Count Stroganov were also present. The endless funeral procession included thousands of civil and military servants, who moved across the icebound Neva river, between the rows of the army men stationed along the route. The Tsar and the grand dukes, all on horseback followed the catafalque. The burial ceremony at SS. Peter & Paul's was not attended by Count Stroganov who was said to remark that with her death died all his feelings. Nor did their daughter Helen attend the rites. Despite her 15 years she was said to be embarrassed by her name and passionately desired the title of Imperial Highness.

Count Stroganov only just outlived his wife. He died on 6 February 1878 and was buried at the Sergiev monastery. The Maryinsky Palace was bequeathed to Maria's sons, who also inherited some 3 million roubles of debt.

DESCENDANTS OF MARIA AND MAXIMILIAN, PRINCES ROMANOVSKY DUKES OF LEUCHTENBERG

Children

Alexandra
D. of Leuchtenberg
(1840—43)

Maria
Pr. Romanovsky
D. of Leuchtenberg
(1841—1914)
⚭ Wilhelm Pr. of Baden
(1829—1897)

Nicholas
Pr. Romanovsky
4th D. of Leuchtenberg
(1843—90)
⚭ N.S. Akinfieva
C. de Beauharnais
(1839—91)

Eugenia
Pr. Romanovsky
D. of Leuchtenberg
(1845—1925)
⚭ Alexander
Pr. of Oldenburg
(1844—1932)

Evguen
Pr. Romanovsky
5th D. of Leuchtenberg
(1847—1901)
⚭ D.K. Opochinina
C. de Beauharnais
(1845—70)
⚭ Z.D. Skobeleva
Ser. Highness
D. of Leuchtenberg
(1856—99)

Sergei
Pr. Romanovsky
D. of Leuchtenberg
(1849—77)

George
Pr. Romanovsky
6th D. of Leuchtenberg
(1852—1912)
⚭ Térèse
Pr. of Oldenburg
(1852—83)
⚭ Anastasia
Pr. of Montenegro
(1867—1935)

Grandchildren

Nicholas
9th D. of Leuchtenberg
de Beauharnais
(1868—1928)
⚭ C. Maria Grabbe
(1869—1948)

George
10th D. of Leuchtenberg
de Beauharnais
(1872—1929)
⚭ Pr. Olga Repnina
(1872—1953)

Darya
C. de Beauharnais
(1870—1931?)
⚭ Pr. Leon Kotchoubey
(1862—1927)
⚭ Baron V. Grävenitz
(1872—1916)

Alexander
Pr. Romanovsky
7th D. of Leuchtenberg
(1881—1942)
⚭ N.N. Caralli
(1883—1964)

Sergei
Pr. Romanovsky
8th D. of Leuchtenberg
(1890—1974)

Helen
(1892—1974)
⚭ Pr. Stephan Tyshkevich

Great-grandchildren

Nicholas
D. of Leuchtenberg
(1896—1937)
⚭ O.N. Fomina
(1898—1921)
⚭ Elisabeth Müller Himler
(b. 1906)

Alexandra
(1895—1969)

Nadezhda
(1898—1962)

Maria
(1907—93)

Serge
D. of Leuchtenberg
(1903—66)
⚭ Anna Naumova
(1903—93)
⚭ Kira Volkova
(1915—?)
⚭ Olga Wickberg
(1926—?)

Maximililan
D. of Leuchtenberg
(1900—06)

Mikhail
D. of Leuchtenberg
(1905—28)

Helen
(1896—1977)

Nathalie
(b. 1900)

Tamara
(b. 1901)

Dmitri
D. of Leuchtenberg
(1898—1972)
⚭ E.A.Arapova
(Chavchavadze)
(1900—91)

Andrey
D. of Leuchtenberg
(1903—19)

Constantine
D. of Leuchtenberg
(1905—83)
⚭ Pr. D.A.Obolensky
(1903—82)

Great-great-grandchildren

Eugenie
(b. 1929)
⚭ Martin V.Bruch
(1914—88)

Nicholas Alexander
v. Leuchtenberg
(b. 1933)
⚭ Anne Christine Buegge
(b. 1936)

- **Nicholas** (b. 1963) v. Leuchtenberg
- **Constantine** (b. 1965) v. Leuchtenberg

- **Maria** (b. 1926)
- **Anna** (b. 1928)
- **Olga** (b. 1931)
- **Nathalie** (b. 1934)

- **Serge** (b. 1955) v. Leuchtenberg
- **Elisabeth** (b. 1957)

- **Helen** (b. 1922)
- **George** v. Leuchtenberg (1927—63)

- **Xenia** (b. 1930)
- **Olga** (b. 1932)

Descendants of Maria and Maximilian, Princes Romanovsky Dukes of Leuchtenberg

Grand Duchess Maria had three daughters and four sons by the Duke of Leuchtenberg. Six surviving children were created Romanovsky princes and princesses. In accordance with an amendment by Nicholas I to the Fundamentals of Legislation of the Empire, Max and his issue received the rights of members of the Imperial House, and the title Highness was theirs in Russia, but they had no rights to allowances from the Appanages. Soon after Duke Maximilian died, his children were made wards, in order to utilize revenues from the Duke's foreign and domestic land property, shares and dividends."Father died in 1852. In order to sever all family connections with Germany, Emperor Nicholas ordered, as agreed with the King of Bavaria, to launch sales of the Eichstätt principality and other Bavarian property, and so, the Romanovsky family name was handed to us",[37] related Nicholas Maximilianovich. Thus, the prophecy of the Duchess Mother Augusta Amalia came true: her grandchildren were made Russian natives.

Irrespective of their father's legacy, each of the Emperor's grandchildren, the Dukes of Leuchtenberg, upon coming of age, were entitled to a substantial amount of money from His Majesty's Own Chancellery. That money was accumulated due to annual investments over a 20 year period, each year on the birthday of HIH of 6, 000 roubles plus State bond dividends. The wardship committee rigidly executed the order of the late Emperor Nicholas. HRH Duchess of Leuchtenberg also dispensed pensions to her grandchildren. This money and family land allowed Max's offspring to survive after the downfall of the Russian Empire.

So what was the fate of the descendants of Maria and Max, the Princes Romanovsky Dukes of Leuchtenberg (de Beauharnais)?

Their daughter HIH Princess Maria Maximilianovna Romanovsky, Duchess of Leuchtenberg ('Marussia', 1841—1914) married H.H.Ludwig Wilhelm, Prince of Baden (1829—97) in 1863. Their children HRH Maximilian Alexander and AHGDH Sophie Marie and their issue represent other European dynasties.

Prince Nicholas Maximilianovich Romanovsky, 4th Duke of Leuchtenberg, 4th Prince de Beauharnais (1843—90), a talented youth, who was educated by the best professors and graduated from university in 1865 became President of the Imperial Mineralogy Society and Honorary President of the Imperial Technological Society. He supervised new geological research and cartography in Russia. A learned man in the field of mineralogy, he published several articles on the newly discovered minerals. He also designated a considerable amount of money as a scholarship, and a special Nicholas-Maximilianovsky medal which was annually conferred on the best researchers in mineralogy, geology and paleontology, beyond Russia's border as well. The curious thing is that such a scholarship which had once been instituted by his grandfather later helped his offspring Constantine to complete his education in Germany in the confused times of the 1930s.

Due to incessant physical training the weakling once destined to be an invalid became an accomplished athlete, described as "extremely strong and adroit, the best horserider and skater in Petersburg, a remarkable shooter, etc."[38] The academician and mineralogist Koksharov, who accompanied Nicholas on his journey to the Urals in 1866, not only praised the young Duke's capacity for work, his simplicity and manner of talking little but sensibly, but also made the following observation: "the Duke's lackey, Stepanov by name... is faithful as a dog to him; and what's more the fellow is rather educated, speaks good French, English, German, and Polish, listened to Hegel, is well versed in politics and admires Katkov".[39]

In his rank as cavalry general Nicholas took part in the Russo-Turkish war of 1877—78, crossing the Balkans under Commander-General Gurko. However, in 1868 he ruined his career after marrying morganatically Nadezhda Akinfieva (née Annenkova, 1840—91), a divorcee, and the former wife of a colonel in the Guards Vladimir Akinfiev. Such a deed caused much pain to his mother and the House: divorcees were not admitted at Court. A year prior to his marriage Nicholas firmly mentioned in a confidential talk that he would in no way obey the monarch's decision in choosing his own bride. The lovers eloped abroad where a modest wedding at an

Orthodox church took place. The church was perpetuated in a painting according to the couple's wish. The picture is in the hands of their descendants living in the USA.

Their marriage was forbidden by the Emperor, and only after 11 years of incessant petitioning was their union regarded as legal, and only in 1879 was Nadezhda created Countess de Beauharnais by the Imperial decree of Alexander II after much delay. A protest by the French ambassador was not taken into account.

The family travelled back and forth throughout Europe from Paris to Rome, until providence made Nicholas the owner of a small estate in Bavaria called Stein. In Stein his two sons were brought up by Russian tutors. This was a golden era in the history of the small Stein castle: each feast turned into another celebration. For a long time after, the neighbours recalled how the Russian mistress of the castle used to go to Paris for her fashionable clothes. A special train was ordered for these expeditions with a salon-car for servants, a stable-railcar for cows and a special platform for hay. It was at this time that the castle was refurbished in NeoGothic style.

A.A.Polovtsov made notes in his diary about the Duke's depression and dope addiction towards the end of his life. Nicholas Maximilianovich died in Paris in late December 1890. He was buried on 12 January 1891, with all the honours due to a prominent scientist and military man, in the Golitsyn chapel of the Sergiev monastery.[40] Upon his death the Russian honours passed to his brother, while the French honours devolved upon his sons Nicholas and George Leuchtenberg-Beauharnais. However, both his sons were granted the title of Duke of Leuchtenberg with the qualification *Serene Highness* by the Imperial decree of Alexander III dated November 1890. Total separation from the Imperial Family was also specified. Nicholas Maximilianovich and his two sons represent the senior branch of the Leuchtenberg-Beauharnais who had issue to be traced in all lines to the present day. This makes for a special story to be told after learning of the destiny of Maria and Maximilian's other children, who represent the junior branch of the Family which was soon to be extinct.

172 E.K.LIPGHART, ***Nicholas Maximilianovich Prince Romanovsky, 4th Duke of Leuchtenberg, 4th Prince de Beauharnais,*** lithograph, late 19C.

174 According to a family legend, the wedding of Nicholas and Nadezhda took place at this Russian Orthodox church abroad. Private collection of the Leuchtenbergs, USA. First publication.

173 **The Stein castle in Bavaria** where Nicholas and his wife Nadezhda had lived as semi-exiles. After both Nicholas and Nadezhda died, the castle passed over to other members of the Bavarian House as had been stated in the will of its previous owner.

175 **Interior** watercolour which is believed to be painted by Duke Nicholas. Private collection of the Leuchtenbergs, USA. First publication.

177 ***Evguen Maximilianovich Prince Romanovsky, 5th Duke of Leuchtenberg*** (Beauharnais). Photo, 1901.

176 V.V.MATEE, ***Princess Eugenia Maximilianovna of Oldenburg,*** née Princess Romanovsky Duchess of Leuchtenberg (Beauharnais), late 19C.

The daughter Princess Eugenia Maximilianovna Romanovsky Duchess of Leuchtenberg, Princess de Beauharnais (1845—1925) married Alexander Prince of Oldenburg, and was famous for her charitable work and as Chairperson of the Artists' Encouragement Society. She inherited the famous portrait of Maximilian by Briullov. The wonderful but tragic portrait of the Duke, worn out with illness, was completed in Madeira in 1849 where both of them were treated for bad health, despatched to St. Petersburg and thrice exhibited in 1850. Soon after the outbreak of the February revolution in 1917, Princess Eugenia, at that time suffering from acute paralysis, was taken from Petrograd to Finland, and later to France. She managed to take a few family portraits and watercolours with her. Thus Briullov's work escaped requisition. The portrait was first purchased from the heirs by the noted Paris dealer S.A.Belitz, and finally entered the private collection of A.V.Mamonov in Brussels. The Oldenburg princes deserve special research.

178 **The mansion on the English Embankment, No 44.** Residence of Evguen and Zina Beauharnais.

The son Evguen Maximilianovich Prince Romanovsky, 5th Duke of Leuchtenberg, Prince de Beauharnais (1847—1901), towards the end of his life as major-general of the entourage, morganatically married Darya Opochinina (1845—70) in 1869, in Florence, thus casting another blow to his mother's heart. Notwithstanding the protest of the French ambassador, his wife was granted the title of Countess de Beauharnais for herself and her issue by the Imperial decree of Alexander II of 1869. That marriage produced only one daughter Darya (1870—1931?), who was known as Dolly Kotchoubey after her marriage; a noted high society beauty, or lioness, as they say in Russia. Countess Darya Evguenievna divorced Leo Kotchoubey in 1911. Their son Evguen Leonovich, Prince Kotchoubey-

Beauharnais (1894—1951) married in Canada, had two daughters and died in Paris in 1951. Darya was married for a second time to Baron Vladimir Grävenitz, captain of the Imperial Navy. As a widow she is believed to have married twice more in later years. Dora, as she was named under the Soviets, worked in the foreign books department of the Public Library in Leningrad and is said to have died in a Stalin labour camp.

In 1878, Evguen married for the second time a woman called Zinaida Skobeleva (1856—99), who was the sister of a prominent general and hero of the Russo-Turkish war of 1877—78. By the Imperial decree of Alexander II of July 1878 she was created Countess de Beauharnais. Evguen was well educated, of kind disposition and poor health. He led a dissolute life, whooping it up drinking in the notorious company of Grand Duke Vladimir and his wife Grand Duchess Maria Pavlovna, Sr. At all appearances, Evguen was rather embarrassed at being regarded as a drunkard and cuckold among the nobility. The Duke's unenviable reputation was much on account of the scandalous infamacy of his beautiful wife Zina Beauharnais who openly flaunted her almost royal indifference to gossip and envy. In 1889, by the Imperial decree of Alexander III, Zinaida was granted the title of the Duchess of Leuchtenberg with the qualification of *Serene Highness ad personam.*

Grand Duke Alexis' love for his relative Zina Beauharnais kept gossip-mongers busy. This grand ducal menage-à-trois was common knowledge in Petersburg and Europe. Evguen was occasionally given a sound thrashing by the Herculean Alexis at the door of his marital bedchamber in his residence on the English Embankment. He tried vainly to complain to the Tsar about his august brother. Grand Duke Alexander Mikhailovich observed that the Grand Admiral Alexis was ready to sacrifice the whole Russian Navy for the sake of the enchanting sensational Zina. Polovtsov noted that Evguen was "a scoundrel without morals, who, along with his wife, indulged in pumping money out of Alexis".[41] The court talebearers spread the news of how Evguen and Zina tried greedily to extract Empress Joséphine's diamonds from their relative Duke Nicholas. Upon Zina's death the apple of discord was gone: Evguen lived mainly in Paris alone, or stayed at Alexis' palace on the Moika river, and was subject to severe depression and loneliness. He had no children from his second marriage. Zinaida was buried at the Alexander Nevsky Lavra. Two years later her husband was buried next to her. In 1908 the Grand Duke Alexis died at his splendid apartment in Paris. His enlisted property included portraits and a marble statue of the infernal Zina, Serene Highness de Leuchtenberg.

179 F.FLAMENT,
Portrait of Darya Evguenievna, (née Duchess of Leuchtenberg) daughter of Evguen by his first marriage (granddaughter of Maria and Maximilian), 1896. State Hermitage, St. Petersburg.

180 V.V.MATEE,
Sergei Maximilianovich Prince Romanovsky, Duke of Leuchtenberg,
late 1870s.

The third son Sergei, Prince Romanovsky, Duke of Leuchtenberg (1849—77), a most gifted boy in art and music, was assigned to serve at the Ministry of Internal Affairs. But he requested to be transferred to the Horse Guards. On 24 August 1877 he was killed in the Russo-Turkish war at Tyrnovo. The day before he had been presented with a gilded piece of arms with the inscription ‘For courage’. On that fatal early morning when he left for reconnaissance at the Turkish camp at Chifflik, he was dreaming of the Cross of St. George having no idea what kind of a cross awaited him so soon. A surgeon extracted a Turkish bullet out of Sergei's head and handed it over to Duke Evguen who accompanied the coffin with the embalmed body to Petersburg. That was the first death of a grandson of the emperor in action. Just a note hitherto has it that 14 members of the House of Romanov took part in that war. Sergei Maximilianovich was buried at SS. Peter & Paul's by his mother side.

George Maximilianovich Prince Romanovsky, 6th Duke of Leuchtenberg de Beauharnais (1852—1912), an aide-de-camp, was first married to Thérèse, Princess of Oldenburg (1852—83). The marriage was discreet (history repeats itself!) and not in Russia, taking place without prior warning. Such a marriage was against the rules of the Orthodox church: Thérèse's brother Alexander Petrovich was already the husband of George's sister Eugenia. Duchess Thérèse died prematurely and was buried at the Sergiev monastery. In 1889 George married Anastasia Nikolayevna (Stana, 1867—1935), daughter of Nicholas I, the King of Montenegro. That family lived at a residence in Sergievsky Street. His mother bequeathed George the family country estate Sergievka. It was namely at George's villa that the Grand Duchesses Militsa and Stana, two sister-princesses of Montenegro[42], introduced Grigory Rasputin to the Tsar's family. On 1 November 1905, Nicholas II noted in his diary that at a tea party at Sergievka with Militsa and Stana they made the acquaintance of one of God's men, Grigory from the Tobolsk gubernia.

High society looked upon Duke George as a silly and swaggering man. He preferred to lead the easy kind of existence abroad for most of the year, delighting in the fame and magnificence of the House of Romanov, and acting as a lavish tipper. His wife Stana divorced him (1906) in order to remarry Grand Duke Nicholas Nikolayevich, Jr. George was buried next to his mother at SS. Peter & Paul's sepulchre.

During the last reign, George's son by his first marriage Prince Alexander Romanovsky, 7th Duke of Leuchtenberg (Sandro, 1881—1942), sublieutenant in the Life Guard Hussars, aide-de-camp to Nicholas II, was popular at Court. On the eve of the 1917 turmoil he luckily sold his house located on the English Avenue. Prince Gabriel Constantinovich observed that Sandro managed to rescue and take abroad many family valuables which had belonged to his grandparents, the portraits and watercolours by V. and Ed. Haue among others. In 1917, Alexander Duke of Leuchtenberg married an ex-ballerina Nadezhda Caralli, a marriage from which there were no children, and died in France in 1942.

182 **The mansion in Sergievsky Street, No 46.** Residence of George and Anastasia, née Princess of Montenegro. After their divorce the house was bought for Grand Duchess Olga Nikolayevna and her husband Peter A. Prince of Oldenburg.

181 **George Maximilianovich Prince Romanovsky, 6th Duke of Leuchtenberg** (Beauharnais). Photo, 1890s.

184 **The house on English Avenue, No 18,** which Sandro bought from the ballerina Mathilde Ksheshinskaya. It had formerly been used by Grand Duke Constantine Nikolayevich to house ex-ballerina Anna Kouznetsova and his illegitimate children by her. The building was damaged during the siege of Leningrad and never regained its original appearance after restoration.

183 **Alexander Georgievich (Sandro) Prince Romanovsky, 7th Duke of Leuchtenberg,** grandson of Maria and Maximilian. Photo, c.1900.

George and Anastasia had two children by their marriage: Sergei Georgievich, Prince Romanovsky, 8th Duke of Leuchtenberg (1890—1974, b. in Peterhof, d. in Rome), a naval officer, unmarried, and Helen (1892—1974) who in 1917 married Count Stephan Tyshkevich. In 1918 in Petrograd, their secretary interceded on their behalf and petitioned Uritski, the formidable KGB Head in Gorokhovaya Street, to release them. He proved that neither of them were registered on the Hereditary Romanov Register. Sergei finally reached the Crimea where he stayed under house arrest at Dulber castle which belonged to Grand Duke Peter Nikolayevich. His mother Anastasia, other Romanovs and the Dowager Empress also stayed at Dulber. Duke Sergei left Russia together with the Dowager Empress Maria Feodorovna aboard the warships which the Allied Forces sent in 1919 to evacuate several other Romanovs from the Crimea. At present the sole descendant in the line is Helen Tyshkevich' daughter Nathalie Ros Marie (b. 1921).

The eldest son of Nicholas Maximilianovich, Nicholas Nikolayevich 9th Duke of Leuchtenberg, 5th Prince de Beauharnais (b. in Geneva in 1868, d. in France in 1928) entered mining college in Paris at his father's will, but after his mother Nadezhda died he came to Russia and began military service in the famous Preobrazhensky regiment. In 1894, he married Maria Nikolayevna Countess Grabbe (1869—1948), having had issue by her four sons and three daughters: Nicholas (1896—1937), Maximilian (1900—06), Sergei (1903—66), Mikhail (1905—28), Alexandra (1895—1960), Nadezhda (1898—1962) and Maria (1907—93). Duke Nicholas resigned and lived with his wife and children in a family mansion on Kameno-ostrovsky Avenue, No 62—64. He inherited the marvellous portraits by the French masters and most of the Dutch paintings, as well as the splendid arms collection which had belonged to his grandfather Maximilian. In 1919, the arms collection was requisitioned and depleted through theft, in which state it was handed over to the Hermitage. In his rank of general, Nicholas resigned. In 1917, he was probably the only member of the General Staff who tried to dissuade Nicholas II from abdication. In the following year, with great difficulty and separately, the family left Russia which was already involved in fratricidal war. Some members departed via Finland and Sweden, others left via the Crimea. Nicholas, Sr., settled on his estate Ruth near Avignon, in the south of France, and embarked upon wine-making. His 'vin Beauharnais' enjoyed wide popularity. In 1928, he died suddenly following the death of Mikhail, his younger son, in a motor accident.

185 **Nicholas Nikolayevich Duke of Leuchtenberg** wearing the uniform of the Don Cossacks regiment. Photo, late 19-early 20C. Private collection of the Leuchtenberg descendants, USA.

186 **Palace of Nicholas Nikolayevich Duke of Leuchtenberg** on Kamenno-ostrovsky Avenue, No 62. The descendants ascertain that it had been purchased by Prince Gorchakov, the guardian of the two Leuchtenberg boys after the death of Nicholas Maximilianovich, for a considerable amount of money which was augmented due to a partial sale of the Munich picture collection.

187 **Nicholas Nikolayevich Duke of Leuchtenberg**
at the time of WW I, General of Headquarters, one of the few people who tried to dissuade the Tsar Nicholas II from abdication.
The Leuchtenberg family lore, USA.

Nicholas's first-born, also named Nicholas Nikolayevich, Jr., Duke of Leuchtenberg, 6th Prince de Beauharnais (1896—1937) fought the Bolsheviks in vain in General Denikin's army, reached Munich via Constantinople, and in 1928 married Elizabeth Müller-Himmler, a girl from near Munich. Always an able musician, he conducted the famous Choir of Don Cossacks in Bavaria. Nicholas, Jr., was buried on the family grounds at the Seeon cemetry, next to other Leuchtenbergs: his brother Maximilian, Duke George and Duchess Olga. It is taken for granted that their graves with Orthodox crosses on them and Russian inscriptions are always well looked after. The living descendants have informed us that at present the German government envisages the restoration of the former ducal castle as an architectural monument.

Nicholas Alexander, Duke of Leuchtenberg, 7th Prince de Beauharnais (b. 1933), son of Nicholas Nikolayevich, lives near Bonn at present and works at the TV centre. He has never visited Russia but has helped to gather material for this book. His two sons Nicholas Maximilian (b. 1963) and Constantine Alexander (b. 1965), the offspring of Maria and Maximilian, reside in the same area.

Many descendants of the third son, Sergei Nikolayevich, Duke of Leuchtenberg (1903—66, b. in Petersburg, d. in the USA), who married three times, from the 1950s live mainly in the USA. His daughter Maria Magdalena who married Joseph de Pasquale, principal violinist of the Philadelphia Orchestra, and lives in Pennsylvania has informed the author: her father Sergei was educated in France and qualified as an electrotechnical engineer, but his fascination with music made him seek another job. At first Sergei worked for a music publishers in Paris, then moved to Leipzig, where they discovered that World War II had broken out. He had to work as an interpreter, first for the Germans, and later for the Americans when their army occupied Leipzig. As soon as the news was revealed that Saxony had passed to the Russian occupying force in accordance with the Yalta agreement, the family decided to escape. The French Red Cross helped the refugees to get to France and join their Naumov grandparents (all four daughters of Sergei and his first wife Anna Naumova were born in France). Later Sergei went to the USA and worked as an instructor at the United States Army School of Languages in California, where in 1957 he became a citizen of the US. His six children by his first and third marriages live in America at present. Sergei's sister Alexandra (formerly Maid-of-Honour of the Empress, who was married first to Prince Melikov, and then to N.Tereshchenko) died in France. His other sister Nadezhda, a concert pianist, who married Alexander Mogilevsky, a concert violinist, died in the USA. Sergei's sister Maria von Mengden recently died in Brazil

188, 189 **Nicholas Duke of Leuchtenberg and his wife Maria Nikolayevna** (née Countess Grabbe) in 17th century costumes (Head of the Strelets, a Boyar lady summer dress), tailored for the famous fancy dress ball in the Winter Palace which took place in February, 1903.

190 **Nicholas, Jr., Sergei and Dmitri,** sons of Duke Nicholas of Leuchtenberg. Photo, c.1926.

191 **Maria Sergeyevna de Pasquale** (née Duchess of Leuchtenberg) at home. In the background one can see pictures of her ancestors including Empress Joséphine.

192 **Maria Sergeyevna,** a descendant of Maria and Maximilian, near her house in Tudor style in Pennsylvania with the author. March, 1994.

193 **The house on the English Embankment, No 22,** residence of George Duke of Leuchtenberg, the then junior captain in the Horse Guards, where his family lived until 1917.

The younger son of Nicholas Maximilianovich, George Nikolayevich 10th Duke of Leuchtenberg (1872—1929, b. in Rome, d. in Seeon), married Princess Olga Repnin-Volkonsky (1872—1953) by whom he had three sons: Dmitri (1898—1972), Andrey (1903—19) and Constantine (1905—83), and three daughters: Helena (1896—1977), Nathalie (b. 1900) and Tamara (b. 1901). All George's family, a junior captain in the Horse Guards, resided happily at No 22 on the English Embankment. George inherited the best Italian masters from his ancestors' Munich collection. From his grandmother he also inherited many valuable paintings and family portraits, such as Maria Nikolayevna's portrait in her Winter Garden by Timothy Neff, and the marble statue depicting her as Venus by the sculptor Christian Rauch.

Duke George, when he resigned from the rank of colonel, preferred to live on the ancestral Seeon estate in Bavaria. The former tiny Benedictine monastery surrounded by lakes and woods instantly turned into a little Russian paradise frequented by many well-known families, such as Enghelhart, Mussin-Pushkin, Yurievsky, Volkonsky, etc., whose entries have survived in the family guest-book 'Chronicle'. The wonderful landscape and superb

194 **George Nikolayevich 10th Duke of Leuchtenberg.** Private collection of the descendants, USA. First publication.

195 **Olga Duchess of Leuchtenberg** (née Princess Repnin) at the costumed ball at the Winter Palace in 1903, wearing a 17th century boyar dress.

196 **The guest-book 'Chronicle' at Seeon.** Commenced in 1894, first entry was by Count Enghelhart mentioning "vanity of vanities". Many noted names emerge, such as their relatives Princes Yuriyevsky Gogo and Olga, Marina Karnovich, the Repnins, and also good friends, the Mussin-Pushkins, Pahlens among others. Guests' entries on the eve of WW I are particularly noteworthy. Unsnobbish poem of teenager Alexandra, a niece of Duke George, describing their past-time.

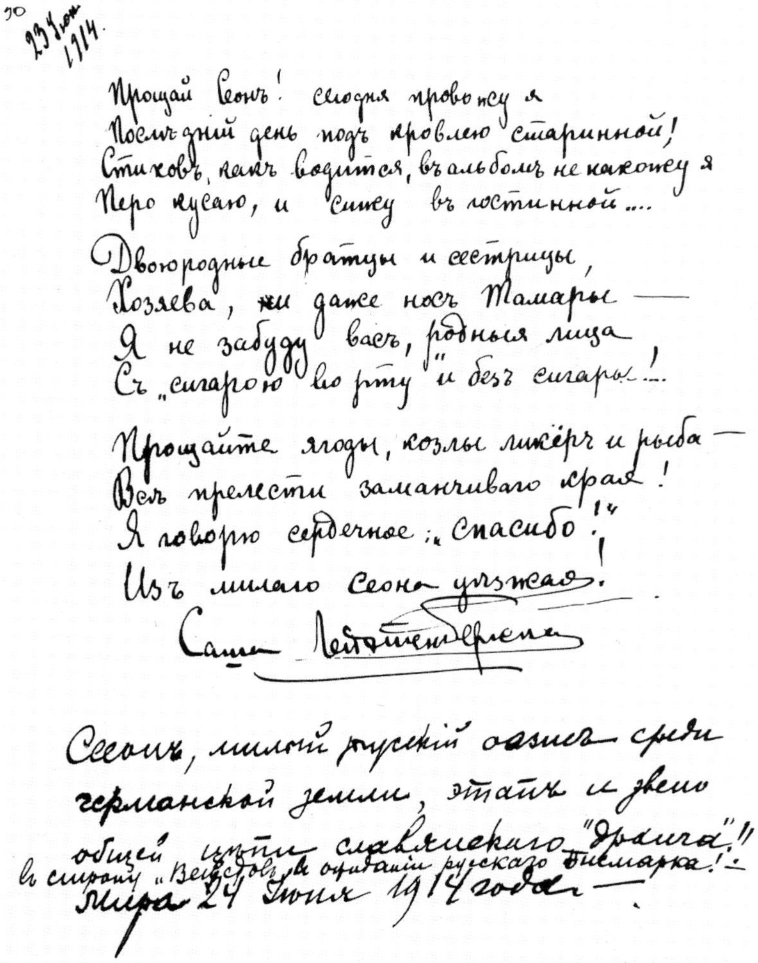

90
23 Iюля 1914.

Прощай Сеонъ! сегодня провожу я
Последний день подъ кровлею старинной;
Стиховъ, какъ водится, въ альбомъ не напишу я
Перо кусаю, и сижу въ гостинной....

Двоюродные братцы и сестрицы,
Хозяева, [illegible] даже носъ Тамары —
Я не забуду васъ, родныя лица
Съ „сигарою во рту" и безъ сигары!...

Прощайте ягоды, козлы ликёръ и рыба —
Всѣ прелести заманчиваго края!
Я говорю сердечное: „Спасибо!"
Изъ милаго Сеона уѣзжая!

Саша Лейхтенбергская

Сеонъ, милой русский оазисъ среди германской земли, этотъ и звено общей цѣпи славянскаго "Drang"!! [illegible]
Мира 24 Iюня 1914 года.

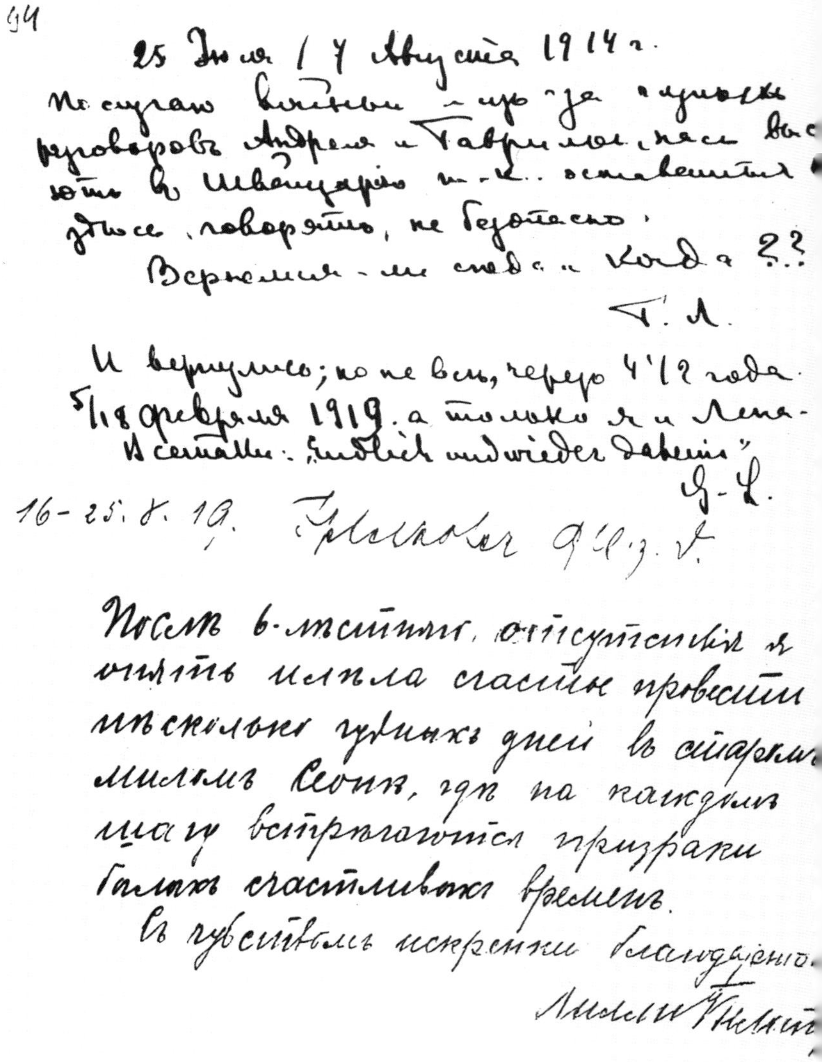

94
25 Iюля / 7 Августа 1914 г.
По случаю войны — из-за глупых разговоров Андрея и Гавриила, нас высылают в Швейцарию т.к. оставаться здесь, говорят, не безопасно.
Вернемся-ли снова и когда??
Г. Л.

И вернулись; но не все, через 4½ года.
5/18 февраля 1919. а только я и Лена.
[illegible]: "Endlich und wieder daheim"
Г. Л.

16–25. 8. 19. [illegible]

После [illegible] отсутствия я опять имела счастье провести несколько тихих дней в старом милом Сеоне, где на каждом шагу встречаются призраки былых счастливых времен.
С чувством искренней благодарности.
[illegible]

197 **Historic entries** signed by George and dated 25 July/7 August 1914 (WW I had just broken out), and the other one dated 5/18 February 1919 which run: "Because of the war and silly chatting of Andrey and Gabriel, we are deported to Switzerland. They say, staying here is unsafe. Shall we ever come back and when?" G.L. "We are back again, four and a half years thenceforth, but not all of us, only Helen and myself managed to come back. And yet, "home, sweet home". A bitter New Year entry by Nicholas: "To make merry at New Year is fine not for the reason that the poor old year is over and the New Year has begun, but one must be happy to have lived through the previous year..." 1 January 1924. Nicholas Leuchtenberg.

organ had once attracted Mozart to stay at the Seeon castle where the composer had planted an oakling. The castle had over 80 rooms. A stuffed brown bear holding honeycomb in its paws, which had once been hunted by Duke Nicholas Maximilianovich in Siberia, welcomed the guests at the grand staircase. The news of the outbreak of World War I reached the family

199 **Small estate Seeon in Bavaria,** 16th century Benedictine monastery, the family property of the Leuchtenbergs, "Russian oasis amidst German lands" in the day of George and Olga. Sold in the 1930s. Currently, an architectural monument & tourist spot.

198, 200 **Graveyard at Seeon** with the graves of Maximilian (1900—06) and Nicholas (1896—1937) Dukes of Leuchtenberg.

201 **Xenia Constantinovna Grabbe** (née v.Leuchtenberg). Photo, 1994. Her seven children and six grandchildren speak Russian.

202 **Xenia Grabbe** visiting Seeon as a tourist. Amama's house had become a hotel, and she was accomodated in a room which had once served as her own bedroom.

there. In August 1914, that news was a thunderbolt to over 100,000 Russians who were relaxing or undergoing medical treatment in Germany at that time, among them several Romanovs.

Here is a story told by Xenia (now an American citizen), granddaughter of George Nikolayevich: “In May 1914, no sooner had Amama returned from Petersburg where the children had to take their examinations for the past year, than a German officer (manoeuvres took place in the woods there) would regularly ask her: ‘Don’t you mean to go to Petersburg?’ Amama seemed to get annoyed by this constant question. After the war was over, they met again and the officer explained his efforts to hint at the necessity for the Leuchtenbergs to leave, without disclosing the top secret of the inevitable war. Grandfather often spent time in the company of German officers who were aware of his Bavarian roots, and he heard them say how fortunate they were that the war had begun in 1914, and not in 1918 as planned: otherwise, Germany would not be able to catch up with Russia’s pace of economic development.”

The family left via Switzerland, where all their valuables were withheld and deposited at a bank. They reached Russia by sea, and stayed in summer with the Repnins, on a grandparent estate in Ukraine. They finally reached Petrograd... to leave again discreetly as refugees. Grandfather (with Helen and Dmitri) left first by a southern route, whilst Grandma (with her other children) was thrown out of her home and forced to huddle in a basement. They were so hungry that father (Constantine) got scurvy which covered his whole body. Their nanny treated the boy with used boiled rice water which she brought from other people. It was Nanny again who found a job for the Duchess and her 13-year-old son in a tomato greenhouse, the owner of which trusted those two workers. He knew they would neither eat nor steal tomatoes. “I was so hungry, so tempted to eat them, but they were not mine”, Constantine recalled... Away from Germany, George did his best to liberate the rest of the family, sparing no money to pay the secret agents who helped the refugees. George Nikolayevich found himself rich: the Swiss banks returned the money and the diamonds of Empress Joséphine. The Germans gave back the Seeon estate which had been requisitioned from the former Russian colonel, who now produced his Ukrainian passport as a result of his association with general Skoropadsky. Being a Ukrainian citizen, George Nikolayevich received Seeon again, where his loyal steward rescued their silver and other valuables cleverly having them immured in the walls. But soon they had to pawn their real estate. Money disappeared immediately: George lent money to new immigrant-businessmen without any guarantee, and gave big sums for the fight against bolshevism. When Constantine finally had a chance to resume his education and enter the Freiburg Academy of Mines to follow in the footsteps of his ancestors, there was no money. Fortunately, the scholarship which had been instituted by his great-grandfather helped indeed... Not all of them came back to Seeon: the family lost 16-year-old Andrey who died of typhoid fever at Narva when guarding the White army railcars as a volunteer.

George Nikolayevich died of cancer of the brain in 1929, on the eve of his son Constantine's marriage to Princess Darya Obolensky. Xenia recollects how seldom her parents had the good fortune to live as a family together: her father qualified as a mining engineer in the mid-1930s, a time of mass unemployment, and he had to sign up for work in South Africa. People who promised him fortunes cheated him, and for over two and a half years her parents never saw each other, having no money to pay the way. And yet, both daughters received a traditional education at home with

203 **Newly-wed** Constantine Duke of Leuchtenberg and Princess Darya Obolensky. Photo, c.1929.

204 **Golden anniversary** of Constantine and Darya Leuchtenberg in Canada. 1979.

205 **Relatives of three generations** celebrate the 50th anniversary.

a governess. For the first time Xenia entered a gymnasium at 11 years of age. The mining engineer Constantine returned to Germany in 1939, but found work only in Austria. The family stayed with grandmother Olga, the last mistress of Seeon. Duchess Olga developed astrakhan production, leased her other house, and was running *Bronze Horseman* Publishing which had been founded by her late husband. (In the 1930s, a time of trouble, the Leuchtenbergs had to sell off the family estate). Only by 1941 the family marked their reunion in Austria. However, four years later they had to run away: in April 1945 the Soviet army gunfire was all too noticeable and the decision was made to go to Bavaria, to Grandma Olga. They lived there for the next 2—3 years, hardly making ends meet, only thanks to books and a vegetable garden. Everybody agreed to move to Canada to join the elder brother Dmitri who had established a winter sports spa in the mountains and a summer travel agency. Constantine found work, first in a remote corner, and finally in the Scientific Translation Service of the Canadian Government in Ottawa where he retired in 1975. Both Constantine and Darya died in Canada, but are buried in Spring Valley, near New York, on the Novodiveyevo convent grounds, where 5 members of the Leuchtenberg family rest: apart from Constantine and Darya, these are his brother Dmitri with his wife Catherine (née Arapov, 1st.marriage Chavchavadze) and the latters' son George.

Nowadays George's descendants live in the US, Canada and France. However, they have taken the family names of their husbands such as Gaydeburoff, Grabbe, Karanfiloff, Ugritschist-Trebinsky, and Meller- Zakomelsky. Helena Dmitrievna became a nun in Bavaria. Alas, members of the grand line of Leuchtenberg-Beauharnais decline in number.

Grand Duchess Maria had a daughter Helen (1861—1908) from her marriage to Stroganov, who married Vladimir Sheremetev (1843—93), from the Moscow gubernia gentry, a Commander of HIM Own Convoy. Helena Grigorievna and particularly her husband enjoyed many favours from the Empress Maria Feodorovna. In 1891, the 'Anichkov favourite' Sheremetev was promoted Major-General of Entourage. They tried to live grandly at their residence at No12 on the expensive English Quay, while receiving subsidies from their relative Eugenia Princess of Oldenburg.[43] Once Sheremetev had squandered all his wife's dowry and other resources, they had to let their house, and received monthly allowances from the Emperor and the Princess of Oldenburg.

The Family and Court could hardly bear the Sheremetev couple. Helen was reputed to be an empty-headed and smooth-tongued gossip, but she was occasionally allowed to say 'thou' to the Emperor. Her husband, a dedicated scoundrel as Polovtsov put it, borrowed money and profiteered on the patronage of his own miserable men by the Empress. Their family inherited a considerable part of Maria Nikolayevna's picture collection. In 1893 Helen's husband died, and she married G.N.Miklashevich, a colonel of HIM Nicholas II's Own Convoy.

After Grand Duchess Maria's death, her sons lived for a short while at the Maryinsky Palace, their notorious life keeping Petersburg agog. Alexander III was very concerned about the scandals plaguing these families. Money was squandered. Soon the Leuchtenbergs were forced to sell off the palace. Polovtsov recalls that there was some crazy idea about installing a kind of night club at the Maryinsky Palace, but reason finally got the upper hand. In 1884, the family palace was sold to the Treasury for three million roubles in order to house there several state offices. That marked the end of the era of palace as family hearth, and thereafter commenced the era of officialdom and civic employees.

Maryinsky Palace during the time of the Imperial Council, and after 1917

In 1885, the palace accomodated the State Council, the Cabinet of Ministers, the State Chancellery (located on the first and upper floors) and the Petitions Chancellery on the ground floor. By order of Tsar Alexander III, the palace retained its old name 'Maryinsky'.

The palace interior was not radically changed. Under the guidance of architect L.L.Peterson it was refurnished and fitted out for its new function. The building seemed enormous to its new inhabitants, and the Imperial Secretary Polovtsov named it a 'Babylonian structure'.

There was an inauguration blessing of the new premises on February 11, 1885. The ceremony began with prayers at St. Nicholas' church and continued into a ceremonial blessing of all the rooms. Four choirs took part, the Imperial choir and that of St. Isaac's among others. All visitors were in full regalia.

And so routine work began. The Rotunda was assigned to a regular sitting of the State Council on Mondays. In those years both the tier cornices were hung with the coats-of-arms of the gubernias (provinces) and the areas of which the Empire was composed. Portraits of the House members were also on the walls. The Square Room was separated from the Rotunda by a heavy velvet curtain. The Duke's Study was used by the Council Chairman. The Concert Hall became a meeting hall of the Cabinet of Ministers. The Oval Room served as a meeting room for the Civic and Ecclesiastic Affairs department. Before endorsement of matters of major importance, all statesmen traditionally would go by ramp to the Church for prayers.

206 **The view of the Maryinsky Palace** and the monument to Emperor Nicholas I in the late 19C. Photo, 1890s.

207 **Study of Grand Duchess Maria** during the time of the Imperial Council. Photo, 1890s.

208 **Bedchamber** of the Grand Duchess during the time of the Imperial Council. Photo, 1890s.

209 **Little Corner Study** of the Grand Duchess during the time of the Imperial Council. Photo, 1890s.

210 I.E.REPIN,
Ceremonial Session of the State Council on 7 May 1901, Celebrating the Centenary of its Foundation,
1903. State Russian Museum, St. Petersburg.

The Ceremonial Session of the State Council centenary which was marked in 1901 is depicted in the renowned painting by Iliya Repin which the artist completed in 1903. The main problem for the celebrated painter was to include 81 participants on the canvas and to place them all only in a favourable position so as not to portray their backs. The last Sovereign Nicholas II presided over that meeting. Sitting on his left was Grand Duke Michael Nikolayevich, a patriarch of the House of Romanov, Chairman of the State Council, and Maria's youngest brother; around the Emperor one can see Maria's nephews, Grand Dukes Vladimir, Serge, Alexis Alexandrovich.

The manifesto of the Tsar dated 17 October 1905 endorsed the State Duma, the lower chamber of Parliament which had its seat at the Tauride Palace. The State Council thus became the upper chamber. Its membership was increased to 215 by the decree of Nicholas II dated 20 February 1906. From that time on, the press and others were admitted to sessions. Therefore a primary objective was to dismantle the central part of the building and sacrifice the Winter Garden for the new Meeting Hall of the State Council.

In January 1907, a special commission launched a contest for the best project to design the Meeting Hall. Four of the eminent architects of the

period were invited to compete: L.N.Benois, A.L.Goon, A.S.Khrenov, and P.I.Shestov. The winning project was that of Leonti Benois. It included the best architectural features already used in public buildings abroad such as the Westminster in England, the Bourbon Palace in France, the Reichstag in Berlin, and the Capitol in America. By the end of 1907, the new huge hall was crowned with an enormous skylight of 182 sq m in area. Both architects L.N.Benois and M.M.Peretiatkovich worked at a great pace and workmen operated round the clock in order to finish the hall by the fixed date of the inauguration of the Council session in October 1908. Iliya Repin's painting was hung right above the Chairman's seat, and was later transferred to the Russian art gallery.

In the political turmoil of the early XX century the Maryinsky Palace became a place of significant events. In April 1902, the Minister of the Interior D.S.Sipiagin was gravely wounded by a revolutionary-terrorist in its vestibule. During the February revolution of 1917 the last sitting of the Council of Ministers took place here under its Chairman Prince N.D.Golitsyn. For a short while after February 1917, the Provisional Government met there, once they had left the Tauride Palace. In autumn 1917, the so-called Pre-Parliament met at the Maryinsky Palace until the Bolsheviks dissolved it.

211 **The new Meeting Hall** for the Imperial Council was installed on the site of the former Winter Garden and adjacent small rooms dismantled in 1907. Iliya Repin's painting was hung right above the Chairman's seat. Photo, 1908.

212 **The Large Meeting Hall** for sessions of the Petersburg Municipal Council. Detail of an enormous skylight of 182 sq m in area. The ceiling was restored after a huge gun shell had destroyed the roof in December 1943.

213 **Detailed capitels and moulded cornice** pattern of the Large Meeting Hall.

After the events of October 1917, the new rulers handed the Maryinsky palace over to the Real Estate Commissariate and the Supreme Soviet of People's Economic Affairs. After the Soviet government left Petrograd for the Kremlin in Moscow in March 1918, the palace housed a number of institutions such as 'Transbalt' (Baltic naval affairs), 'Sevzapvod' (North-west rivers), and the Press House. In 1928—29 a holding agency 'Soviet Tourist' set up a hostel with 1, 000 beds in the ceremonial rooms, where nails were driven into walls in order to hang topcoats and dry underwear, and where footwear was thrown around on precious inlaid floors.

For 10 years (1929—39) the Stalin Industrial Academy used the building for its students, dormitories, classrooms and for staff lodgings. The walls of the rooms were covered with planks and coated with cheap wallpaper, and the marble columns and window bays were painted in oil. In 1940, the Higher Communist party school began operating a course there.

The new hosts changed the interior by removing the two-headed eagles and coats-of-arms and replacing them with five point stars and slogans. The Register of 1940 relates that a few statues have their noses broken, and a few murals are gone. The most appalling damage was wrought to St. Nicholas' Church. The communion table, the altar and icons disappeared, biblical murals were damaged when they were plastered over, and the church stairwell was repainted. However, in 1938 some restoration work started in several rooms.

During the Second World War the palace was used as a hospital. The siege of Leningrad in 1941—44 ensured great damage to the building: it was hit by two shells and received nearly forty incendiary bombs. On 6 December 1943, a big gun shell destroyed the roof of the Meeting Hall.

The war was not yet over when in 1944 rapid conservation works began on the edifice. In 1946 they patched the roofing, had the engineering system restored, and commenced the restoration of the gala rooms and the servants' quarters. Overall repairs were carried out under the architect M.A.Shepelevski.

From 1945, the Maryinsky Palace became the headquarters of the Executive Committee of the Leningrad City Soviet, serving in effect as the town hall. This initiated not only the first post-siege restoration but also some rebuilding of the palace. Alterations began in 1945 on the east wing: a new marble staircase was installed, and the former guest room area was redesigned. Once again the Church was irrevocably damaged: the skylight was removed and closed with a cast-iron plinth which supported a flag pole to fly a banner over the building. The green marble fireplace and the lionesses disappeared out of the Entrance Hall. Replicas of five medals and orders won by Leningrad for military and labour exploits were displayed at the front of the attic. These replicas, electronic clocks, and slogans somehow distorted the façade of the building by diminishing its royal grandeur.

From the late 1960s onwards the scheduled scientific restoration was aimed at the removal of all room decor which had distorted the palace's original character. Thus the Pompeian Gallery murals were restored, and in 1975 the complex restoration of the former State Reception Room and the Ball Room was carried out. The frieze paintings by A.Vighi were cleaned and hidden behind new paintings by the Soviet artist V.A.Serov who produced three mediocre compositions on the history of the city. Dried and cracked in the siege period the inlaid doors caused a particular problem. Painting of the upper part of the Square Room was badly damaged by leakages causing dirty spots, paint decay, and holes in the painted cloth.

In the Church none of the mural paintings by Gagarin has survived completely. With painful care restorers cleaned the walls by hand, inch by inch and cleansed and uncovered about 15% of the authentic painting. After the war the Church had been used as a cinema, and the Oratory as a projector room. In 1990, the Church was restored and consecrated, and for the first time in 73 years believers began to worship there.

At present, the newly elected municipal administration is housed in the palace.

The Maryinsky Palace maintains a remarkable position among the eternal architectural masterpieces of St. Petersburg. It constantly revives the memory of its former owners and is a wonderful example of harmony and beauty. They deserve all our gratitude. Not only for their deeds, but also for the construction of this lavish palace abounding in the richest collections of national and world art which has augmented Russia's national wealth and guaranteed the ex-owners a permanent place in history. It is with great shame and distress we have to admit that all the family graves in Petersburg and in its environs; Maria's and the Duke's, their children and grandchildren; all have been damaged, robbed, and desecrated.

It is high time to pay tribute not in word but in deed to the architect Stakenschneider and to revive his marble bust which by order of Grand Duchess Maria, was immediately erected in Stakenschneider's lifetime in one of the halls as a token of her gratitude for such a wonderful building.

NOTES

1 According to the Act on the Imperial Family issued by Emperor Paul I on 5 April 1797, Grand Dukes/Duchesses were the descendants (sons, daughters, grandsons, greatgrandsons) of the reigning or deceased emperor. Yet, in 1886 Emperor Alexander III restricted the title of Grand Duke/Duchess to the sons/daughters, and to the grandsons in the male line.
2 Tsesarevich was brought up and educated together with Ioseph Wielgorsky and Alexander Patkul who were his age, because his own brothers were much younger.
3 Hertsen, A. I., Byloe i dumi. p. 72
4 Adalbert, prinz, Die Herzen... S. 161
5 Same. S. 200
6 Same. S. 197
7 Custine, Marquis de, Nikolayevskaya Rossia, p. 461, 462
8 Rossia... glazami inostrantsev, p. 668, 670
9 Hagern, F. Zapiski. Rossia i Russki dvor v 1839 g. //Russkaya starina. 1890. Feb, p. 327
10 Punin, A. L., Arkhitektura Peterburga... p. 83
11 Sankt-Peterburgskiye Vedomosti. 1845. Feb, No35, p. 151
12 Opis naruznomu pandusu pri strojachemsa v SPb Dvortse Yeja Imperatorskovo Vysochestva Velikoy Knjagini Marii Nikolayevni 12 janvaria 1845, RGIA, fond 542, delo 70, p. 151
13 Illustratsia. 1845. t. 1, No1, p. 5
14 Sollogub, V. A., Vospominania... p. 55
15 Smirnova, A. O. (Rossette), Avtobiografia. p. 114
16 Kelly, L. St. Petersburg. p. 75
17 Anna F. Tiutcheva(1829—89), daughter of Russian poet F.I. Tiutchev, a talented memorialist. Stayed at Court for 13 years. Governess of Alexander II's children: Maria, and later Serge and Paul.
18 Tiutcheva, A. F. Pri dvore... p. 24
19 Illustratsia. 1845. v. 1, No2, p. 17
20 Illustratsia. 1845, v. 1, No2, p. 18
21 After Emperor Paul I was murdered in a plot (12 March, 1801) the former Michael Castle was neglected. From 1819 it housed the Military Engineering School, and part of the old decor became useless. In 1843, Nicholas I visited the Castle and ordered the transfer of a few doors into the Maryinsky Palace.
22 Peterburgsky Listok. 1885, No39. 11 Fevr. p. 2
23 Same
24 Loranski, A., Istoricheski ocherk Gornogo instituta. SPB. 1873. p. 122
25 Tiutcheva, A. F. Pri dvore... p. 24
26 Adalbert, prinz, Die Herzen... S. 240
27 Adalbert, prinz, Die Herzen... S. 348
28 Adalbert, prinz, Die Herzen... S. 345
29 Tiutcheva, A. F. Pri dvore... p. 24
30 Andrey, one of three sons of the historian N. Karamzin. He was clever, handsome and a great success in high society. Married Aurora K. Demidova, a beautiful and rich widow.
31 Polovtsov, A. A. Dnevnik... v. 1, p. 462
32 Tiutcheva, A. F. Pri dvore... p. 109
33 E.I.V. Kniaz Nikolai Maximilianovich. Ocherk moyevo detstva i yunosti//Russkaya starina. 1890. mai, p. 478
34 Same. p. 480
35 Same p. 477
36 Valuev, P. A. Dnevnik. p. 337
37 E.I.V. Kniaz Nikolai Maximilianovich. Ocherk... p. 479
38 Belogolovy, N.A.Vospominaniya. SPB,1901, p.452—495
39 Same, p. 454
40 Trinity-St. Serge monastery near Strelna, founded in 1735 by Varlaam, Father-Superior of Trinity — St. Serge Lavra, in the reign of Empress Anna Ioannovna. Construction thereat was carried out by architects P. Trezzini, L. Rusca, A. Stakenschneider, A. Gornostayev. Architect A. Stakenschneider was buried there.
41 Polovtsov, A. A. Dnevnik... v. 1, p. 396
42 Princesses Militsa (1866—1951) and Anastasia (1868—1935), daughters of Nicholas I, King of Montenegro, married Grand Duke Peter Nikolayevich and George Maximilianovich Duke of Leuchtenberg
43 Polovtsov, A. A. Dnevnik... v. 2, p. 9

SELECT BIBLIOGRAPHY

Александр Михайлович, великий князь. Книга воспоминаний. М., 1991
Анненкова А.К. Воспоминания//Наша старина, 1915, т. 2—4
Барановский Г.В. Архитектурная энциклопедия второй половины XIX века. СПб, 1904, т. IV
Бенуа А.Н., Лансере Е.Н. Дворцовое строительство императора Николая I // Старые годы, 1913, №7—9
Белоголовый Н.А. Воспоминания и др. статьи. СПб, 1901
Буранов Ю., Хрусталев В. Гибель Императорского дома. М., 1992
Вальден П.И. Очерк истории химии в России. Одесса, 1917
Весь Петербург. Адресный справочник за 1890—1917гг.
Воронов Н.И. Воспоминания об императоре Николае I и его семье// Исторический вестник, 1908, т. 114, №11
Врангель Н.Н.Наследие великой княгини Марии Николаевны. СПб, б. д.
Гавриил Константинович, вел.кн. В Мраморном дворце. Нью-Йорк, 1955
Гагерн Ф. Россия и русский двор в 1839 г.//Русская старина. 1890, февр.
Герцен А.И. Былое и думы. М., 1960
Глинский Б.Б. Революционный период русской истории (1861—1881). Исторический очерк. СПб, 1913,ч.1,2
Грабарь И.Э. История русского искусства. М., 1912, т. 3
Гримм А. Императрица Александра Федоровна//Отечественные записки, 1866, т. 166, №6
Дневник П.А.Валуева, министра внутренних дел. М., 1961, т. 1, 2
Дневник Д.А.Милютина. М.,1949, т.2
Дом Романовых. СПб, 1992
Зильберштейн И.С. Парижские находки. М., 1993
Кедринский А.А. и др. Восстановление памятников архитектуры Ленинграда. Л., 1987
Кокшаров Н.И. Воспоминания. 1818—1859//Русская старина, 1890, №6
Крашенинников А.Ф. Мариинский дворец. Л., 1964 (ГИОП, рукопись)
Кукольник Н.В. Мариинский дворец // Иллюстрация, 1845, т. 1, №1, 2
Кюстин де.маркиз. Николаевская Россия. М., 1930
Лакруа Поль. Черты из жизни и царствования императора Николая I. СПб, 1869
Львов Л. За кулисами старого режима. Воспоминания журналиста. Л., 1928
Лонгинов М.Н. Заметки о петербургских дворцах//Русский архив, 1873, кн. 1
Месяцослов. СПб, 1839, 1846
Мещерский В.П. Мои воспоминания. СПб, 1897, т. 1—3
Мосолов А.А., генерал. При дворе последнего императора. СПб, 1992
Некрасов И. Молельня при церкви Мариинского дворца в Санкт-Петербурге. М., 1867
Неустроев А.А. Собрание картин герцога Г.Н.Лейхтенбергского. СПб, 1904
Николай Михайлович, великий князь. Некрополь. СПб, 1912, т. 2
Петербургские страницы воспоминаний графа Соллогуба с портретами его современников. СПб, 1993
Паткуль М.А. Воспоминания// Исторический вестник, 1902, т. 87
Петрова Т.А. Андрей Штакеншнейдер. Л., 1978
Половцов А.А.Дневник Государственного секретаря. М., 1966, т. 1, 2
Пунин А.Л. Архитектура Петербурга середины XIXвека. Л., 1990
Пыляев М.И. Старый Петербург. СПб, 1912
Россия 1-й половины XIX века глазами иностранцев. Л., 1991
Русский биографический словарь. СПб, 1892
Смирнова, А.О. (Россет). Автобиография. М., 1931
Столпянский П.Н. Старый Петербург и Общество поощрения художеств. Л., 1928
Татищев С.С. Император Александр II, его жизнь и царствование. СПб, 1903, т. 1,2
Тютчева А.Ф. При дворе двух императоров. М., 1990
Фредерикс М.В. Воспоминания// Исторический вестник, 1898, май
Шильдер Н.К. Император Николай I. СПб, 1903, т. 1, 2
Штакеншнейдер Е.А. Дневник и записки. М.—Л., 1934
Эйсснер А. А.И.Штакеншнейдер// Зодчий, 1902, №12, 14

Российский государственный исторический архив, ф. 542, дела 10, 15, 58, 70
Центральный государственный архив Октябрьской революции, ф. 115, оп. 11, д. 7, 25, 27, 3565—3575
Adalbert v.Bayern, Prinz, *Die Herzen der Leuchtenberg*, München 1963
Burke's Peerage, *Royal Families of Europe*, London 1977
Chavchavadze, David, *The Grand Dukes*, New York 1990
Fanning, Charles, *The Dukes of Leuchtenberg*, London 1983
Ferrand, Jacques. *Romanoff. Un album de famille*, Paris 1989
Ferrand, Jacques. *Romanoff. Un album de famille* — Compliment. Paris 1990
Kelly, Laurence, *St.Petersburg*, London 1981
Michael, Prince of Greece, *Imperial Palaces of Russia*, London 1992